The Jefferson Bible

THE JEFFERSON BIBLE

THE LIFE AND MORALS OF JESUS OF NAZARETH

THOMAS JEFFERSON

With an Introduction by F. Forrester Church
and an Afterword by Jaroslav Pelikan

BEACON PRESS · BOSTON

Beacon Press
25 Beacon Street
Boston, Massachusetts 02108

Beacon Press books
are published under the auspices of
the Unitarian Universalist Association of
Congregations.

96 95 94 93 92 91 90   8 7 6 5 4 3

LIBRARY OF CONGRESS CATALOGING-IN-PUBLICATION
DATA
Jefferson, Thomas, 1743–1826.
The Jefferson Bible / The life and morals of Jesus of
Nazareth;
with an introduction by F. Forrester Church and an
afterword by Jaroslav Pelikan.
p.   cm.
English, French, Greek, and Latin.
Originally published: Washington, D.C. : U.S. G.P.O.,
1904.
Includes index.
ISBN 0-8070-7701-1
1. Jesus Christ—Rationalistic interpretations.
2. Bible. N.T. Gospels—Criticism, interpretation,
etc.   3. Jesus Christ— Biography—Sources, Biblical.
4. Jesus Christ—Teachings.   5. Jesus Christ—History
of doctrines—18th century.   6. Jesus Christ—History of doctrines—19th century. 7. Bible. N.T. Gospels—Criticism, interpretation, etc.—18th century.   8. Bible. N.T. Gospels—Criticism,
interpretation, etc.— History —19th century.
I. Bible. N.T. Gospels.   II. Title.
BT304.95.J44   1989
226'.1—dc 19   88-34447

Contents

Following page 32 of "The Gospel according to Thomas Jefferson" appear facsimiles of three pages from Jefferson's own compilation: (1) the title page; (2) page 60, showing Jefferson's arrangement of the parallel passages in Greek, Latin, French, and English; (3) the first page of Jefferson's Table of the Texts.

Preface

In 1956, my father, Frank Church, won election to the United States Senate. As had been the custom since 1904, on the day of his swearing in he was presented with copy of Thomas Jefferson's Bible, *The Life and Morals of Jesus of Nazareth*. Two years later he gave the book to me.

On first reading, even to the eyes of a ten-year-old boy, Jefferson's Bible struck with the force of unexpected revelation. For instance, there was no mention of virgin birth or resurrection. From my occasional bouts with Sunday school, I knew how the Jesus story was supposed to begin (with angelic visitations and an immaculate conception), and end (the empty tomb and ascension to heaven). Being skeptical by nature and upbringing, such miracles figured prominently in my resistance to this great story's saving power. Jefferson's *Life and Morals of Jesus of Nazareth* began to change all that. A redaction of the four Gospels (Jefferson cut out and pasted together only those passages that made sense to him), his Bible unlocked the Scriptures for me, opening up a whole new world, one I have been exploring with deepening wonder ever since.

When my father gave me Thomas Jefferson's Bible, he quoted a famous passage from one of Jefferson's letters; "It is in our lives and not our words that our religion must be read." This led to our first serious discussion of religion; it also marked the first time religion made any sense to me. Later, when I sat down and actually read *The Life and Morals of Jesus of Nazareth*, I encountered a savior who was born in the usual way and died in the usual way. By Jefferson's reading, it was Jesus' unusual life on earth—made unusual by the simple eloquence of his teachings—that truly mattered. Though I have developed a deeper appreciation for the Gospels in their received form than Jefferson had, this put a bold new spin on the question of redemption, one that has stayed with me. I define religion as our human response to the dual reality of being alive and having to die. Resurrection or no resurrection, Jesus triumphed over death: he lived in such a way that his life proved worth dying for.

With the gift of Jefferson's Bible, a door opened for me that ultimately led to a vocation in religion. At Harvard Divinity School I wrote my master's thesis on Thomas Jeferson's Bible, under the supervision of George Huntston Williams, a Unitarian minister and church historian. In 1978 I completed a doctorate in religion at Harvard University, and was called to the ministry of All Souls Unitarian Church in New York City, where I have served ever since. Some thirty years ago, when I opened *The Life and Morals of Jesus of Nazareth*, I had no idea that Jefferson espoused a Unitarian theology, or that he once claimed that "there is not a young man now living in the U.S. who will not die an Unitarian." But in retrospect I can see that the seed of a faith that has been growing ever since was then planted in the mind of a ten-year-old boy.

You can imagine, therefore, what pleasure I take in introducing Jefferson's Bible to you. With the exceptions of an expensive scholarly edition and a gift-shop pocket version sold at Monticello, *The Life and Morals of Jesus of Nazareth* has been out of print, and therefore unavailable, for years. I am so very grateful to Wendy Strothman, director of Beacon Press, for welcoming my suggestion that Beacon republish a new edition of Jefferson's Bible, and delighted that she asked Professor Jaroslav Pelikan of Yale University to join with me in introducing it. Ten years ago Dr. Pelikan wrote an essay for my first publishing venture, *Continuities and Discontinuities in Church History: Essays in Honor of George Huntston Williams on His Sixty-fifth Birthday*, which I co-edited with Timothy George (Leiden: Brill, 1978). The opportunity to work with Dr. Pelikan again on a text that I first devoted careful attention to as Dr. Williams's student, represents one of those little continuities that invest my life with meaning and joy.

F. FORRESTER CHURCH

THE GOSPEL ACCORDING TO
Thomas Jefferson

F. FORRESTER CHURCH

On 17 July 1771, his neighbor Robert Skipwith asked Thomas Jefferson to propose a list of books suitable for a library befitting the dignity of a Virginia gentleman. Skipwith was prepared to invest some twenty-five or thirty pounds; he wished to have his volumes finely bound and gold-embossed. Jefferson promptly drew up a catalog of books, plainly bound, costing no less than one hundred and seven pounds, and then suggested, not unkindly, that Skipwith instead abandon the scheme, and come to his home, "the new Rowanty, from which you may reach your hand to a library formed on a more extensive plan."

When Jefferson offered the same opportunity to Congress in proposing to sell his library to replace that which had been destroyed by fire by the British during the War of 1812, Congressman Cyrus King of Massachusetts was offended. From the floor of the House he exclaimed: "It might be inferred, from the

1

character of the man who collected it, and France, where the collection was made, that the library contained irreligious and immoral books, works of the French philosophers, who caused and influenced the volcano of the French Revolution. The bill would put $23,999 into Jefferson's pocket for about 6,000 books, good, bad, and indifferent, old, new, and worthless, in languages which many cannot read and most ought not."

More telling than King's invective was Jefferson's scheme of classification as formulated in the catalog that he submitted to Congress. Building upon the framework that Francis Bacon in 1605 had constructed in his essay, "The Advancement of Learning," Jefferson classified his books with reference to the processes of mind employed on them: (1) *Memory*, which is applied to factual data, such as "History"; (2) *Reason* (according to Bacon, *Understanding*), which is applied to theoretical investigations, such as "Philosophy"; and (3) *Imagination*, which is applied to innocent pleasures, such as the "Fine Arts." But having appropriated Bacon's three principal divisions of learning, Jefferson further adapted them to conform with modern canons of epistemology. Under "Philosophy," of the two primary subdivisions—"From Reason" and "Revealed"—only the former remains, no longer identified as such, but assumed to be guiding the "Moral" and "Mathematical" pursuits into which it has been divided. As additional evidence for the changes Jefferson worked upon Bacon's categories, "Mathematical" had previously been a third-tier subsection of "Metaphysics/Speculative"; "Natural Religion," which had stood in its place (having first been transformed by Jefferson into "Law of Nature and Nations"), now served to fill the lacuna left by "Mathematics" on the lowest rank.

One could go on, but for our purposes it need only be pointed out that Jefferson subtended "Religion" to "Jurisprudence," a category of "Philosophy/Moral," where its awkwardness suggests that he had been reluctant to ascribe to it an autonomous, if more appropriate, status. In addition, Jefferson demoted "Ecclesiastical History" from a partner to a function of "Civil History," while eliminating its more speculative subdivisions, such as "History of Providence."

To substantiate any conclusions one might draw from such schemes of subordination, we need only look to Jefferson's breakdown of authors and titles under the various headings. Since his library catalog reflects the same fundamental principles of classification illustrated by the list of books he had proposed to Skipwith, by turning to this we may gain a clearer notion of Jefferson's criteria. To Skipwith, under "Religion" and shouldering Sterne's sermons, Jefferson commended Xenophon on Socrates, Epictetus, Antoninus, Seneca, Cicero, and, of the moderns, Lord Kames's *Natural Religion*, Bolingbroke, and Hume. Classified under ancient history, together with Bayle's *Dictionary* and Plutarch's *Lives*, are Caesar, Livy, Sallust, Josephus, Tacitus, *and* the Bible.

JEFFERSON'S "SYLLABUS"

As a young man, Jefferson had been much taken by the philosophical writings of Henry St. John, Viscount Bolingbroke. Though a Tory in politics, Bolingbroke's religious skepticism proved sufficiently engaging to prompt Jefferson to record passages from Bolingbroke's writings into his "Literary Bible," a commonplace book composed during the 1760s and early 1770s. Not only do the quotations from Bolingbroke constitute by far the most extensive entry (some sixty handwritten pages), but they are also the only ones to treat Christianity explicitly. As an indication of Jefferson's own early thinking on the subject of religion, one passage of Bolingbroke's that he chose to reproduce in his commonplace book is particularly telling.

4

It is not true that Christ revealed an entire body of ethics, proved to be the law of nature from principles of reason, and reaching all the duties of life.... Were all the precepts of this kind, that are scattered about in the whole new testament, collected, like the short sentences of ancient sages in the memorials we have of them, and put together in the very words of the sacred writers, they would compose a very short as well as unconnected system of ethics. A system thus collected of the writings of ancient heathen moralists, of Tully, of Seneca, of Epictetus, and others, would be more full, more entire, more coherent, and more clearly deduced from unquestionable principles of knowledge.

If Jefferson had been convinced of this in his youth, by 1803 he had begun to adjust his opinions. Although admitting that the teachings of Jesus were incomplete and had suffered badly at the hands of those who had edited them, Jefferson was now prepared to claim that the fragments remaining showed a master workman, whose "system of morality was the most benevolent and sublime ... ever taught, and consequently more perfect than those of any of the ancient philosophers." We must look to the years between for evidence that may help explain Jefferson's change of heart.

In the evenings of 1798–99, when he was John Adams's vice president, Jefferson engaged Dr. Benjamin Rush in a series of "delightful conversations ... which served as an anodyne to the afflictions of the crisis through which our country was then laboring." The Christian religion was sometimes their topic, and in the course of one discussion Jefferson promised Rush, a doctor from Philadelphia, well-respected scientist, and outspoken Universalist, that one day he would write down his view of it. In September of 1800, Jefferson wrote Rush to assure him that he had not forgotten his promise. "On the contrary," he explained, "it is because I have reflected on it, that I find much more time necessary for it than I can at present dispose of." For the moment he could only say, "I have a view of the subject which ought to displease neither the rational Christian nor Deist, and would reconcile many to a character they have too hastily rejected. I do not know that it would reconcile the *genus irritabile vatum* who are all in arms against me. Their hostility is on too interesting ground to be softened."

Jefferson was then standing as a candidate for the presidency. It was natural that his thoughts, in turning to religion, would fix on certain sectaries, the more vocal of whom were reviling him as an infidel too impious to be president. "The returning good sense of our country threatens abortion to their hopes," Jef-

ferson wrote to Rush. "They believe that any
portion of power confided to me, will be ex-
erted in opposition to their schemes. And they
believe rightly; for I have sworn upon the altar
of God, eternal hostility against every form of
tyranny over the mind of man."

The following spring, a triumphant Jefferson
ascribed to his victory legendary proportions.
"It was the Lilliputians upon Gulliver," he
wrote. "Our countrymen have recovered from
the alarm into which art and industry had
thrown them; science and honesty are replaced
on their high ground; and you, my dear Sir, as
their great apostle, are on its pinnacle." This
"great apostle" was Dr. Joseph Priestley, promi-
nent scientist and Unitarian theologian.

Men like Benjamin Rush and Joseph Priestley
helped to reestablish Christianity as a viable
option for "reasonable" and "enlightened" re-
publicans such as Thomas Jefferson. Historian
J. B. Bury, in developing his special theme (the
idea of progress), cited Priestley's doctrine of
historical progress as a "solvent of theological
beliefs" heralding the French philosopher Au-
guste Comte's Religion of Humanity. Rush,
whose principal contribution to American
thought was made in chemistry and medicine,
also proved an ardent champion of theological
openness. Urging his fellow Universalists to es-

chew sectarian association and include persons of every Christian society into their fellowship, he sought the establishment of an ecumenical body that would serve the interests of many in a shared and single cause. Like Priestley, Rush too believed that "all truths are related, or rather there is but one truth." As he wrote to the Reverend Jeremy Belknap in 1791, "Republicanism is a part of the truth of Christianity. It derives power from its true source. It teaches us to view our rulers in their true light. It abolishes the false glare which surrounds kingly government, and tends to promote the true happiness of all its members as well as of the whole world, for peace with everybody is the true interest of all republics." If Rush, a political ally and trusted friend, prompted Jefferson to consider incorporating a constructive Christian philosophy into his thought, Priestley suggested the means by which he might do it. By consulting the annals of history, Priestley had determined that much of Christian doctrine was either defiant of or superfluous to the Christian message. The Gospel was therefore not only obscured, but also distanced from the lives of many persons who had neither the time nor the means to investigate it properly.

Four years passed before Jefferson found the time to fulfill his promise to Rush. "The more

I considered it, the more it expanded beyond the measure of either my time or information," Jefferson explained. But one day, as he was about to return to Washington from an early spring visit to Monticello, inspiration knocked. In the mail, Jefferson received from Joseph Priestley his short treatise, *Socrates and Jesus Compared.* Otherwise unoccupied for the return trip, he had occasion to peruse it. Finding the contents supportive of his own tentative conclusions, he wrote Priestley an enthusiastic reply. Alluding in the course of this letter to his promise to Rush, Jefferson sketched the form that the fulfillment of that promise might take:

I should proceed to a view of the life, character, and doctrines of Jesus, who sensible of the incorrectness of his forbears' ideas of the Deity, and of morality, endeavored to bring them to the principles of a pure deism, and juster notions of the attributes of God, to reform their moral doctrines to the standard of reason, justice, and philanthropy, and to inculcate the belief of a future state. This view would purposely omit the question of his divinity, and even his inspiration. To do him justice, it would be necessary to remark the disadvantages his doctrines had to encounter, not having been committed to writing by himself, but by the most unlettered of men, by memory, long after they had heard them from him, when much was forgotten, much misunderstood, and presented in every paradoxical shape. Yet such are the fragments remaining as to show a master workman, and that his system of morality was the most benevolent and sublime probably that has been ever taught, and consequently more perfect than those of any of the ancient philosophers. His character and doctrines have received still greater injury from those who pretend to be his special disciples, and who have disfigured and sophisticated his actions and precepts, from views of personal interest, so as to induce the unthinking part of mankind to throw off the whole system in disgust, and to pass sentence as an imposter on the most innocent, the most benevolent, and the most eloquent and sublime character that ever has been exhibited to man.

Jefferson drew up his *Syllabus of an estimate of the merit of the Doctrines of Jesus, compared with those of others* sometime during the two weeks following his letter to Priestley. An enlargement upon the outline there suggested, he sent it to Benjamin Rush in fulfillment of their long-standing agreement. Four years had passed, during which, Jefferson claimed, "At the short intervals ... when I could justifiably abstract my mind from public affairs, the subject has been under my contemplation." As he had before to Priestley, Jefferson explained how, in time, his conception of the task had outdistanced his ability to accomplish it. In lieu of something more substantial, he sent his *Syllabus* to Rush, "as the only discharge of my promise I can probably ever execute."

Divided into three sections, "Philosophers," "Jews," and "Jesus," Jefferson articulated his thesis more explicitly than he had in the letter to Priestley. Of Jesus, he wrote:

1. Like Socrates & Epictetus, he wrote nothing himself.

2. But he had not, like them, a Xenophon or an Arrian to write for him. On the contrary, all the learned of his country, entrenched in its power and riches, were opposed to him, lest his labors should undermine their advantages; and the committing to writing his life and doctrines fell on the most unlettered and ignorant men; who wrote, too, from memory, and not till long after the transactions had passed.

3. According to the ordinary fate of those who attempt to enlighten and reform mankind, he fell an early victim to the jealousy and combination of the altar and the throne, at about 33 years of age, his reason having not yet attained the maximum of its energy, nor the course of his preaching, which was but of 3 years at most, presented occasions for developing a complete set of morals.

4. Hence the doctrines which he really delivered were defective as a whole, and fragments only of what he did deliver have come to us mutilated, misstated, and often unintelligible.

5. They have been still more disfigured by the corruptions of schismatising followers, who have found an interest in sophisticating and perverting the simple doctrines he taught by engrafting on them the mysticisms of a Grecian sophist, frittering them into subtleties, and obscuring them with jargon, until they have caused good men to reject the whole in disgust and to view Jesus himself as an imposter. Notwithstanding these disadvantages, a system of morals is presented to us, which, if filled up in the true style and spirit of the rich fragments he left us, would be the most perfect and sublime that has ever been taught by man.

In his cover letter to Rush, Jefferson described his *Syllabus* as "the result of a life of inquiry and reflection, and very different from the anti-Christian system imputed to me by those who know nothing of my opinions. To the corruptions of Christianity, I am indeed opposed; but not to the genuine precepts of Jesus himself."

Having fulfilled his promise to Rush, Jefferson turned again to Priestley. Convinced that Priestley would act upon any suggestion he might make, Jefferson commended his proposed study of Jesus' doctrines—as outlined in his *Syllabus*—to Priestley's care. That December, when Priestley agreed to investigate the matter further, Jefferson was delighted. "I have prevailed upon Priestley to undertake the work," Jefferson wrote to his daughter, Mary. "He says he can accomplish it in the course of a year." The only stumbling block was Priestley's health. "In truth his health is so much impaired," Jefferson admitted, "and his body become so feeble, that there is reason to fear he will not live out even the short term he has asked for it." A month later, in renewing his support and appreciation, Jefferson wrote to Priestley, "I rejoice that you have undertaken the task of comparing the moral doctrines of Jesus with those of the ancient Philosophers. You are so much in possession of the whole subject, that you will do it easier and better than any other person living." The letter was probably not seen by Priestley, who died within a week of its posting.

In this final letter to Priestley, Jefferson included one further bit of advice concerning Jesus, which he expected Priestley to accept without question. "I think you cannot avoid giving, as preliminary to the comparison, a digest of his moral doctrines, extracted in his own words from the Evangelists, and leaving out everything relative to his personal history and character. It would be short and precious. With a view to do this for my own satisfaction, I had sent to Philadelphia to get two testaments Greek of the same edition, and two English, with a design to cut out the morsels of morality, and paste them on the leaves of a book, in the manner you describe as having been pursued in forming your Harmony. But I shall now get the thing done by better hands."

The first intimation of Jefferson's Bible, this passage also reflects a gap between Jefferson's perception of Priestley and Priestley himself. Though both were Unitarian in theology, Priestley was far more reverent toward the Evangelists' record of Jesus' teachings than Jefferson was. Had Priestley compiled such a digest, it likely would have included every saying of Jesus recorded by the Evangelists, with the possible exception of duplications. What Jefferson failed to recognize was that, whereas Priestley doubted the genuineness of certain phenomena suggested by Scripture, he did so by showing them to be secondary to the original accounts of the Evangelists. To Priestley, the Evangelists were inspired, accurate, and trustworthy. The culprits were not Matthew, Mark, Luke, and John, but later writers, who somehow managed to graft their own speculations onto the Scriptures. Accounts of the virgin birth, for instance, clearly cut against Priestley's sense of the historical grain, but given that the story was missing from Mark, he simply concluded that the first chapters of Matthew and Luke could accordingly be dismissed as interpolations.

In exposing the corruptions of Christianity, Priestley was defending the purity of the scriptural witness. In reviling the credulous for accepting on faith unreasonable manifestations of the Spirit in later times, he was protecting the special authority of the wonderworkers whose deeds were authoritatively attested in the Testaments, Old and New. To Jefferson, on the other hand, the Evangelists were ignorant, unlettered men. If they were guilty of considerable presumption in proposing to record Jesus' life and teachings, one would be even more presumptuous uncritically to accept their accounts. Had Priestley lived, Jefferson would surely have been disappointed by Priestley's fidelity to the Evangelists' accounts of Jesus' life and teachings. But Priestley did not live, and so Jefferson determined to accomplish on his own the task he was certain Priestley would otherwise have performed to their mutual satisfaction: he himself would try his hand at cutting up the Gospels.

Shortly before importuning Priestley, Jefferson had written to a Philadelphia bookseller for duplicate copies of both the English and the Greek New Testament. The English edition was the King James translation published by Jacob Johnson in Philadelphia in 1804; the Greek, Wingrave's printing of Leusden's Greek Testament, published in London in 1794. Whether or not Jefferson intended it, the Greek text came with a parallel Latin translation (done in "a very dubious kind of Latin," in one scholar's estimation) that proved to be the work of Benedictus Arias Montanus, the Spanish editor of the Antwerp polyglot of 1569–72. Though Jefferson had expressed an interest only in the Greek with an English translation facing, when the Bibles arrived in three versions, he appears to have determined, for the sake of symmetry, to incorporate also a French translation. A year after Priestley's death, on 31 January 1805, Jefferson ordered two copies of "le Nouveau Testament corrigé sur le Grec," identical with the Paris Ostervald edition, published in 1802 under the auspices of the British and Foreign Bible Society in London. By mid 1805 Jefferson was thus in possession of the makings of his four-column *Life and Morals of Jesus of Nazareth.* The six books sat untouched on his shelves for fifteen years.

THE PHILOSOPHY OF JESUS
OF NAZARETH

The most mysterious chapter in the story of
Jefferson's Bible concerns his first actual ab-
straction of Jesus' words from the four Gospels.
Entitled *The Philosophy of Jesus of Nazareth*, this
little work is first mentioned in a letter to John
Adams dated 13 October 1813.

We must reduce our volume to the simple evangelists,
select, even from them, the very words only of Jesus,
paring off the amphiboligisms into which they have
been led, by forgetting often, or not understanding
what had fallen from him, by giving their own mis-
conceptions as his dicta, and expressing unintelligibly
for others what they had not understood themselves.
There will be found remaining the most sublime and
benevolent code of morals which has ever been offered to man. I have performed this operation for my
own use, by cutting verse by verse out of the printed
book, and by arranging the matter which is evidently
his, and which is as distinguishable as diamonds in a
dunghill. The result is an octavo of forty-six pages, of
pure and unsophisticated doctrines, such as were pro-
fessed and acted on by the unlettered Apostles, the
Apostolic Fathers, and the Christians of the first century.

When did Jefferson perform this operation,
and what has *The Philosophy of Jesus* to do with
Jefferson's designs of 1803–5? The evidence

from his correspondence is sketchy. "I have made a wee little book," he wrote in 1816 to his old friend, Charles Thompson, "which I call the Philosophy of Jesus. It is a paradigma of his doctrines, made by cutting the texts out of the book, and arranging them on the pages of a blank book, in a certain order of time or subject. A more beautiful or precious morsel of ethics I have never seen." A somewhat more precise reference to Jefferson's *Philosophy* appears three years later in a letter to William Short, a Unitarian with whom Jefferson maintained a correspondence concerning religion during his final years. Describing it as an "Abstract from the Evangelists of whatever has the stamp of the eloquence and fine imagination of Jesus," Jefferson reports that he attempted the task "too hastily some 12. or 15. years ago. It was the work of 2. or 3. nights only at Washington, after getting thro' the evening task of reading the letters and papers of the day." A record of his receipts indicates that Jefferson was not exaggerating. On 4 February 1804, two New Testaments (nearly identical editions published in Dublin by George Grierson in 1791 and 1799) arrived from his bookseller; little more than a month later, on March 10, Jefferson's finished work returned from the bindery.

On the cover page, Jefferson described the

contents as "an abridgment of the New Testament for the use of the Indians, unembarrassed with matters of fact or faith beyond the level of their comprehensions." As this ascription of purpose is not to be reiterated, much less elaborated, in any subsequent mention of the *Philosophy*, one must entertain it with caution. In no way is it impossible that Jefferson should have sponsored such a project. In 1809 he greeted a secular plan for civilizing the Indians as "undoubtedly a great improvement on the ancient and totally ineffectual one of beginning with religious missionaries." Once the Indians had been taught to raise cattle, to reckon value, to keep accounts, and to read, only then, stated Jefferson, should the missionaries be brought in. "Our experience has shown that this must be the last step of the process," Jefferson wrote. In the "final quarter's" instruction, Jefferson's ideal curriculum for the education of Indians might well have included an expurgated account of Jesus' doctrines.

But the evidence suggests that, when he prepared *The Philosophy of Jesus*, Jefferson's mind was more on himself than on the Indians. When alluding to the *Philosophy* in his correspondence, never once did Jefferson describe it as a collection for the Indians. "I have performed this operation for my own use," he wrote in a letter to Adams. On another occasion, Jefferson spoke of the project as an extension of ideas contained in the *Syllabus* made "for my own satisfaction." One possibility is this: in his reference to "the Indians" Jefferson was wryly alluding to his Federalist opponents. He had done so at least once before, in his second inaugural address. There he veiled a critique of his political and religious opponents with reference to the "prejudices" of the aboriginal inhabitants of America. A more likely explanation is simply that, being extremely wary of any public discussion of his private religious feelings, Jefferson was providing himself with a cover story should his *Philosophy* ever come to public notice.

In either case, Jefferson clearly viewed the *Philosophy* as but the partial fulfillment of a promise, one to be completed in *The Life and Morals of Jesus of Nazareth*, a late and, by that time, unexpected fruit of his old age. That he had intended to expand his *Philosophy* earlier, recasting it in a format that would accommodate Greek, Latin, and French texts in parallel with the English, is clear from his ordering of two French New Testaments in January 1805. But the stimulus was gone. Remember, Jefferson made his first cut at the Gospels within a week or two of hearing of Joseph Priestley's death. A

20

year later, without Priestley to fire it further, his passion began to fade. By mid 1805, when the final set of Testaments arrived from Philadelphia, the motivation necessary to complete the work was gone. Wanting the provocation of a correspondent, Jefferson could not sustain his interest in the project. Had it not been for John Adams, who began to prod him in a remarkable correspondence initiated a decade later, *The Life and Morals of Jesus of Nazareth* would have remained an unfulfilled dream.

THE ADAMS CORRESPONDENCE

Before his letter of September 1800 to Benjamin Rush, Jefferson's published correspondence contains only one extended reference to his religious beliefs. But in the wake of his promise to Rush, a dozen more followed in the space of three and a half years, each alluding to reflections evoked by it. It is therefore fitting that after almost ten years of silence the subject of Jefferson's religious opinions again came to the fore on the occasion of Rush's death. Saddened by the loss of a close and beloved friend, Jefferson was also concerned lest, in the sorting of Rush's papers, his *Syllabus* should arouse curiosity and be indiscreetly used. To Benjamin's son, Richard, Jefferson wrote:

My acquaintance with him began in 1776. It soon became intimate, and from that time a warm friendship has been maintained by a correspondence of unreserved confidence. In the course of this, each had deposited in the bosom of the other communications which were never intended to go further. In the sacred fidelity of each to the other these were known to be safe: and above all things that they would be kept from the public eye. There may have been other letters of this character written by me to him: but two alone occur to me at present, about which I have any anxiety. These were of April 21, 1803 and January 16, 1811. The first of these was on the subject of religion, a subject on which I have ever been most scrupulously reserved. I have considered it as a matter between every man and his maker in which no other, and far less the public had a right to intermeddle. To your father alone I committed some views on this subject in the first of the letters above mentioned, led to it by previous conversations, and a promise on my part to digest and communicate them in writing.

Jefferson wrote this letter on 31 May 1813. Amplifying his fears, only nine days later he discovered that one of his letters to Joseph Priestley had been published without authorization in another's memoirs. The bearer of this distressing news was none other than John Adams. On this ironic note began the notable correspondence between Jefferson and Adams on the subject of religion.

While reading *The Memoirs of Theophilus Lindsey*, a British Unitarian minister, Adams happened upon Jefferson's letter to Priestley of 1803, the one in which he described his compact with Rush and commended his proposed outline of Jesus' doctrines to Priestley's care. Assuming that Jefferson had not fulfilled his pledge to Rush, Adams wrote to him, "Your letters to Priestley have increased my grief, if that were possible, for the loss of Rush. Had he lived, I would have stimulated him to insist on your promise to him, to write him on the subject of religion. Your plan I admire." Having done what he could to cajole Jefferson into contemplating such matters anew, Adams closed by announcing, "I have more to say on this subject of religion."

Two days later Adams made good on this boast. His opening salvo to Jefferson on the subject of religion is littered with credentials: the names of divines and philosophers and their books, many "whose titles you have never seen." Superficially, it appears that an insecure Adams was seeking to impress Jefferson with the breadth of his knowledge. More likely he was simply pledging his openness, his willingness to listen, his childlike delight in variety. All is summed up in Adams's closing statement: "I think I can now say I have read away bigotry, if not enthusiasm."

In the third letter of twice as many days, Adams stated his purpose clearly: "I hope you will still perform your promise to Doctor Rush." Two weeks later he reiterated that hope, including excerpts of Priestley's letter of 19 December 1803 to Lindsey, in which Priestley discusses the project suggested to him by Jefferson. "I send you this extract for several reasons," Adams wrote. "First, because you set him upon this work. Secondly, because I wish you to endeavor to bring it to light and get it printed. Thirdly, because I wish it may stimulate you to pursue your own plan which you promised to Dr. Rush."

On 22 August, Jefferson finally responded. "Since my letter of June the 27th, I am in your debt for many; all of which I have read with infinite delight. They open a wide field for reflection, and offer subjects enough to occupy the mind and pen indefinitely." Jefferson was particularly pleased by Adams's approval of his outline to Priestley. "Your approbation of my outline to Dr. Priestley is a great gratification to me," he wrote. The case was again open.

Adams's prodding brought Jefferson's *Life and Morals of Jesus of Nazareth* one step closer to fruition.

THE LIFE AND MORALS OF
JESUS OF NAZARETH

How and when Jefferson finally created *The Life and Morals of Jesus of Nazareth* is nowhere made explicit. The *Philosophy* was first mentioned during the correspondence with Adams, and then again in the letter to Charles Thompson in January of 1816. In the spring of that same year, Francis Adrian van der Kemp, a Dutch scholar and Unitarian minister, having been shown the *Syllabus* when visiting John Adams, wrote to Jefferson inquiring after it. At some point during this same period, Jefferson seems to have recommitted himself to his original task.

"If I had time," Jefferson wrote to Charles Thompson, "I would add to my little book the Greek, Latin and French texts, in columns side by side." That was in January of 1816. By April of the same year, Jefferson had elected the coming winter as the time during which he would complete his design. "It was too hastily done," he wrote, "... being the work of one or two evenings only, while I lived at Washington, overwhelmed with other business, and it is my intention to go over it again at more leisure. This shall be the work of the ensuing winter."

Failing to find time for it that winter, Jefferson seems, once again, to have abandoned any hope of completing his design. Three years later, he wrote to William Short, "These are now idle projects for me. My business is to beguile the wearisomeness of declining life, as I endeavor to do, by the delights of classical reading and of mathematical truths, and by the consolations of a sound philosophy, equally indifferent to hope and fear."

Whatever drove him out of his idleness long enough, first to revise the *Philosophy*, and further, to cut out the passages and paste them in a book, is nowhere made explicit. Most scholars give 1819 as the probable time of its execution, but given Jefferson's mood of late October that year, this is less likely than a subsequent date. For a more reasonable estimate, we must turn to Jefferson's additional correspondence with Short.

One hypothetical reconstruction of the chronology is as follows. As was the case before with Priestley, Adams, and Van der Kemp, upon learning of Jefferson's *Syllabus*, his friend William Short requested a copy in March 1820. Responding to this request, Jefferson had occasion to review the *Syllabus*, and consequently to assess its inadequacy as a guide for his present thoughts. He then determined to revise the *Philosophy*, partly to clarify in his own mind which of the sayings extracted before from the Gospels would survive a more deliberate scrutiny. He was well advanced in this process by the thirteenth of April, when he forwarded the *Syllabus* to Short. In the body of the covering letter, for the first time in sixteen years he spoke of restoring the Scriptures to their original purity, without expressing dissatisfaction with his first attempt (or even mentioning it), as had heretofore been his custom in correspondence whenever the subject arose. In addition, Jefferson now distanced himself from the opinions of Jesus as outlined in the *Syllabus*, indicating a new flurry of activity and reflection. In his covering letter, he wrote to Van der Kemp:

While this syllabus is meant to place the character of Jesus in its true and high light, as no imposter Himself, but a great Reformer of the Hebrew code of religion, it is not to be understood that I am with Him in all His doctrines. I am a Materialist; He takes the side of Spiritualism. He preaches the efficacy of repentance towards forgiveness of sin; I require a counterpoise of good works to redeem it, etc., etc. It is the innocence of His character, the purity and sublimity

of His moral precepts, the eloquence of His inculca-
tions, the beauty of the apologues in which He con-
veys them, that I so much admire; sometimes, indeed,
needing indulgence to eastern hyperbolism. My eu-
logies, too, may be founded on a postulate which all
may not be ready to grant. Among the sayings and
discourses imputed to Him by His biographers, I find
many passages of fine imagination, correct morality,
and of the most lovely benevolence; and others,
again, of so much ignorance, so much absurdity, so
much untruth, charlatanism and imposture, as to
pronounce it impossible that such contradictions
should have proceeded from the same Being. I separate, therefore, the gold from the dross; restore to
Him the former, and leave the latter to the stupidity
of some, and roguery of others of His disciples.

Jefferson's opinions on Jesus and the Evangelists are sharper than ever before. Judging
from the rhetoric of his letters, he is increasingly impatient with Jesus' biographers, yet his
selections in this second compilation are more
encompassing of biographical details in Jesus'
life. These two developments—Jefferson's
growing distrust of the Evangelists' account and
his growing interest in Jesus' life as well as his
teachings—began with the Adams correspondence of 1813–14. This led to his decision to
revise the *Philosophy* in 1816, and culminated,
most likely, during the spring of 1820 with the
composition of the *Life*. This last conjecture is

based upon the second and third of Jefferson's letters to Short. As can be seen from the passage just cited, we meet a significant change of tense in those sentences that describe the process of extraction: "I find, ... separate, ... restore, ... leave." One senses here either present or recent involvement in the task.

In a third letter to Short, mailed on 4 August, there is even stronger evidence that the work has finally been done and is fresh in mind.

We find in the writings of [Jesus'] biographers matter of two distinct descriptions. First, a groundwork of vulgar ignorance, of things impossible, of superstitions, fanaticisms and fabrications. Intermixed with these, again, are sublime ideas of the Supreme Being, aphorisms, and precepts of the purist morality and benevolence, sanctioned by a life of humility, innocence, and simplicity of manners, neglect of riches, absence of worldly ambition and honors, with an eloquence and persuasiveness which have not been surpassed. These could not be the intentions of the groveling authors who related them. They are far beyond the powers of their feeble minds. They show there was a character, a subject of their history, whose splendid conceptions were above suspicion as being interpolations from their hands. Can we be at a loss in separating such materials and ascribing each to its original author? The difference is obvious to the eye and to the understanding, and we may read as we run to each his part; and I will venture to affirm that he who, as I have done, will undertake to winnow this grain from the chaff, will find it not to require a moment's consideration. The parts fall asunder of themselves, as would those of an image of metal and clay.

Here Jefferson can look back upon a work accomplished, not one hastily completed some sixteen years before, with which he was no longer pleased. The memories are fresh, the product satisfying. In 1820, at seventy-seven years of age, Thomas Jefferson removed the six testaments from his shelf, where they had been sitting for a decade and a half, and carved out a Gospel for himself, one whose witness he could respect and whose message he could understand.

Thomas Jefferson's interest in the Bible was restricted entirely to the life and teachings of Jesus. Eloquent, benevolent, innocent, a victim first of the Roman state and then of the Christian church, Jesus was the lamb whom humankind would never tire of slaughtering. In a statement of his faith, Jefferson wrote to Rush, "I am a Christian, in the only sense he wished any one to be; sincerely attached to his doctrines, in preference to all others; ascribing to himself every human excellence; and believing he never claimed any other." Historian Daniel

J. Boorstin notes, "The Jeffersonian had projected his own qualities and limitations into Jesus, whose career became his vivid symbol of the superfluity and perils of speculative philosophy."

As with many Unitarians of like spirit who have followed him, Jefferson's was a search not so much for the historical as for the intelligible Jesus. John Adams recognized it as such in 1813 when he wrote to Jefferson, "I admire your employment in selecting the philosophy and divinity of Jesus, and separating it from all mixtures. If I had eyes and nerves I would go through both Testaments and mark all that I understand." Which is precisely what Thomas Jefferson did, not once but twice, with the Gospels.

The

Life and Morals

of

Jesus of Nazareth

Extracted textually

from the Gospels

in

Greek, Latin

French & English.

28 Καὶ προσελθὼν εἷς τῶν γραμματέων, ἀκούσας αὐτῶν συζητούντων, εἰδὼς ὅτι καλῶς αὐτοῖς ἀπεκρίθη, ἐπηρώτησεν αὐτόν· Ποία ἐστὶ πρώτη πασῶν ἐντολή;

29 Ὁ δὲ Ἰησοῦς ἀπεκρίθη αὐτῷ· Ὅτι πρώτη πασῶν τῶν ἐντολῶν· Ἄκουε Ἰσραὴλ, Κύριος ὁ Θεὸς ἡμῶν, Κύριος εἷς ἐστι.

30 Καὶ ἀγαπήσεις Κύριον τὸν Θεόν σου ἐξ ὅλης τῆς καρδίας σου, καὶ ἐξ ὅλης τῆς ψυχῆς σου, καὶ ἐξ ὅλης τῆς διανοίας σου, καὶ ἐξ ὅλης τῆς ἰσχύος σου· αὕτη πρώτη ἐντολή.

31 Καὶ δευτέρα ὁμοία αὕτη· Ἀγαπήσεις τὸν πλησίον σου ὡς σεαυτόν. μείζων τούτων ἄλλη ἐντολὴ οὐκ ἔστι.

40 Ἐν ταύταις ταῖς δυσὶν ἐντολαῖς ὅλος ὁ νόμος καὶ οἱ προφῆται κρέμανται.

32 Καὶ εἶπεν αὐτῷ ὁ γραμματεύς· Καλῶς, διδάσκαλε, ἐπ' ἀληθείας εἶπας ὅτι εἷς ἐστι Θεός, καὶ οὐκ ἔστιν ἄλλος πλὴν αὐτοῦ·

33 Καὶ τὸ ἀγαπᾶν αὐτὸν ἐξ ὅλης τῆς καρδίας, καὶ ἐξ ὅλης τῆς συνέσεως, καὶ ἐξ ὅλης τῆς ψυχῆς, καὶ ἐξ ὅλης τῆς ἰσχύος, καὶ τὸ ἀγαπᾶν τὸν πλησίον ὡς ἑαυτόν, πλεῖόν ἐστι πάντων τῶν ὁλοκαυτωμάτων καὶ τῶν θυσιῶν.

Κεφ. κγ. 23.

1 Τότε ὁ Ἰησοῦς ἐλάλησε τοῖς ὄχλοις καὶ τοῖς μαθηταῖς

2 λέγων· Ἐπὶ τῆς Μωσέως καθέδρας ἐκάθισαν οἱ γραμματεῖς καὶ οἱ Φαρισαῖοι·

3 Πάντα οὖν ὅσα ἂν εἴπωσιν ὑμῖν τηρεῖν, τηρεῖτε καὶ ποιεῖτε· κατὰ δὲ τὰ ἔργα αὐτῶν μὴ ποιεῖτε· λέγουσι γάρ, καὶ οὐ ποιοῦσι.

4 Δεσμεύουσι γὰρ φορτία βαρέα καὶ δυσβάστακτα, καὶ ἐπιτιθέασιν ἐπὶ τοὺς ὤμους τῶν ἀνθρώπων· τῷ δὲ δακτύλῳ αὐτῶν οὐ θέλουσι κινῆσαι αὐτά·

5 Πάντα δὲ τὰ ἔργα αὐτῶν ποιοῦσι πρὸς τὸ θεαθῆναι τοῖς ἀνθρώποις· πλατύνουσι δὲ τὰ φυλακτήρια αὐτῶν, καὶ μεγαλύνουσι τὰ κράσπεδα τῶν ἱματίων αὐτῶν·

6 Φιλοῦσί τε τὴν πρωτοκλισίαν ἐν τοῖς δείπνοις, καὶ τὰς πρωτοκαθεδρίας ἐν ταῖς συναγωγαῖς.

---

28 Et accedens unus Scribarum, audiens illos conquirentes, videns quod pulchre illis responderit, interrogavit eum: quod esset primum omnium mandatum?

29 At Jesus respondit ei, quia primum omnium mandatorum: Audi Israël, Dominus Deus noster, Dominus unus est.

30 Et diliges Dominum Deum tuum ex toto corde tuo, & ex tota anima tua, & ex tota cogitatione tua, & ex tota virtute tua. Hoc primum mandatum.

31 Et secundum simile huic: Diliges proximum tuum ut teipsum. Majus horum aliud mandatum non est.

40 In his duobus mandatis universa Lex & Prophetæ pendent.

32 Et ait illi Scriba: Pulchre Magister in veritate dixisti, quia unus est Deus, & non est alius præter eum.

33 Et diligere eum ex toto corde, & ex toto intellectu, & ex tota anima, & ex tota fortitudine: & diligere proximum ut seipsum, plus est omnibus holocautomatibus, & sacrificiis.

CAPUT XXIII.

1 Tunc Jesus loquutus est turbis, & discipulis.

2 Dicens: Super Mosi cathedram sederunt Scribæ & Pharisæi:

3 Omnia ergo quæcumque dixerint vobis servare, servate & facite: secundùm verò opera eorum ne facite: dicunt enim, & non faciunt.

4 Alligant enim onera gravia & importabilia, & imponunt in humeros hominum: at digito suo non volunt movere ea.

5 Omnia verò opera sua faciunt adspectari hominibus, dilatant verò phylacteria sua, & magnificant fimbrias vestimentorum suorum.

6 Amantque primos recubitus in cœnis, & primas cathedras in synagogis.

28. Alors un des Scribes , qui les avoit ouï disputer ensemble, voyant qu'il leur avoit bien répondu , s'approcha, et lui demanda : Quel est le premier de tous les commandemens?

29. Jésus lui répondit : Le premier de tous les commandemens est celui-ci : Ecoute Israël, le Seigneur notre Dieu est le seul Seigneur.

30. Tu aimeras le Seigneur ton Dieu , de tout ton cœur, de toute ton ame , de toute ta pensée , et de toute ta force. C'est là le premier commandement.

31 Et voici le second , qui lui est semblable : Tu aimeras ton prochain comme toi - même. Il n'y a point d'autre commandement , plus grand que ceux-ci.

40. Toute la loi et les Prophètes se rapportent à ces deux commandemens.

32. Et le Scribe lui répondit : Maître, et tu as bien dit , et selon la vérité , qu'il n'y a qu'un seul Dieu, et qu'il n'y en a point d'autre que lui ;

33. Et que l'aimer de tout son cœur , de toute son intelligence , de toute son ame , et de toute sa force, et aimer son prochain comme soi-même , c'est plus que tous les holocaustes et que tous les sacrifices.

Alors Jésus parla au peuple , et à ses Disciples,

2. Et leur dit : Les Scribes et les Pharisiens sont assis sur la chaire de Moyse.

3. Observez donc , et faites tout ce qu'ils vous diront d'observer ; mais ne faites pas comme ils font; parce qu'ils disent et ne font pas.

4. Car ils lient des fardeaux pesans et insupportables , et les mettent sur les épaules des hommes ; mais ils ne voudroient pas les remuer du doigt.

5. Et ils font toutes leurs actions, afin que les hommes les voient ; car ils portent de larges phylactères , et ils ont de plus longues franges à leurs habits ;

6. Ils aiment à avoir les premières places dans les festins , et les premiers sièges dans les Synagogues ;

28 And one of the scribes came, and having heard them reasoning together, and perceiving that he had answered them well, asked him, Which is the first commandment of all ?

29 And Jesus answered him, The first of all the commandments is, Hear, O Israel; The Lord our God is one Lord :

30 And thou shalt love the Lord thy God with all thy heart, and with all thy soul, and with all thy mind, and with all thy strength: This is the first commandment.

31 And the second is like, namely this, Thou shalt love thy neighbour as thyself. There is none other commandment greater than these.

40 On these two commandments hang all the law and the prophets.

32 And the scribe said unto him, Well, Master, thou hast said the truth : for there is one God ; and there is none other but he:

33 And to love him with all the heart, and with all the understanding, and with all the soul, and with all the strength, and to love his neighbour as himself, is more than all whole burnt-offerings and sacrifices.

CHAP. XXIII.

The Pharisees exposed, &c.

THEN spake Jesus to the multitude, and to his disciples

2 Saying, The scribes and the Pharisees sit in Moses' seat:

3 All therefore whatsoever they bid you observe, *that* observe and do; but do not ye after their works: for they say and do not.

4 For they bind heavy burdens and grievous to be borne, and lay *them* on mens' shoulders; but they *themselves* will not move them with one of their fingers.

5 But all their works they do for to be seen of men: they make broad their phylacteries, and enlarge the borders of their garments.

6 And love the uppermost rooms at feasts, and the chief seats in the synagogues.

A Table

of the Texts of this harmonized from the Eva
employed in this Narrative
and of the order of their arrangement.

2. 1—7. Joseph & Mary go to Bethlehem, where Jesus is b
21. 39. he is circumcised & named & they return to Nazar
40. 42—48. 51. 52. at 12. years of age he accompanies
parents to Jerusalem and returns.

1. 2. Mk. 1. & M. 3. 4. 5. 6. John baptises in Jordan.

21. 22. Jesus is baptised. L. 3. 23. at 30. years of age.

2. 12—16. drives the traders out of the temple.

M. 4. 12. Mk. 6. 17—28. he baptises but retires into Galilee on the death of

Mk. 1. 21. 22. he teaches in the Synagogue.

12. 1—8. 9—12. Mk. 2. 27. M. 12. 14. 15. explains the Sabba

L. 6. 12 — 17. call of his disciples.

M. L. 6. 24. 25. 26. M. 5. 13—47. L. 6. 34. 35. 36. M. 6. 1—34.

L. 6. 20. M. 7. 3—20. 12. 35. 36. 37. 7. 24—29. the Sermon in the Mo

Mk. 2. & Mk. 6. 6. M. 11. 28. 29. 30. exhorts.

L. 7. 36—46. a woman anointeth him.

Mk. 3. 31—35. L. 12. 1—7. 13—15 precepts

L. 12. 16. —21. parable of the rich man.
L. 13. 1—5
22—48. 54. 59. precepts.

L. 13. 6—9. parable of the figtree.

L. 14. 37—46. 52. 53. 54. precepts.

M. 13. 1—9. Mk. 4. 10. M. 13. 18—23. parable of the Sower

Mk. 4. 21. 22. 23. precepts. M. 13. 24—30. 36—52. parable of the

Mk. 4. 26—34. L. 9. 57—62. L. 5. 27—29. Mk. 2. 15—17. precepts
L. 5. 36—39. , parable of new wine in old bottles.

M. 13. 53—57. a prophet hath no honor in his own country.

M. 9. 36. Mk. 6. 7. M. 10. 5. 6. 9—18. 22. 26—31. Mk. 6. 12. 30. mission, instru,

L. 7. 1. Mk. 7. 1—5. 14—24. M. 15. 1—2. 7—9. 12—17. 21—28. 5 precepts

M. 18. 23. — 35. parable of the wicked servant.

A TABLE of the Texts from the Evangelists employed in this Narrative and of the order of their arrangement.

*[1] **Luke 2.** 1-7. Joseph & Mary go to Bethlehem, where Jesus is born.

21. 39. he is circumcised & named & they return to Nazareth.

40. 42-48. 51. 52. at 12 years of age he accompanies his parents to Jerusalem

[2] and returns.

L. 3. 1. 2. **Mk. 1.** 4. **Mt. 3.** 4. 5. 6. John baptises in Jordan.

Mt. 3. 13. Jesus is baptised. **L. 3.** 23. at 30 years of age.

[3] **J. 2.** 12-16. drives the traders out of the temple.

J. 3. 22. **Mt. 4.** 12. **Mk. 6.** 17-28. he baptises but retires into Galilee on the death of John.

[4] **Mk. 1.** 21. 22. he teaches in the Synagogue.

[5] **Mt. 12.** 1-5. 9-12. **Mk. 2.** 27. **Mt. 12.** 14. 15. explains the Sabbath.

L. 6. 12-17. call of his disciples.

[6] **Mt. 5.** 1-12. **L. 6.** 24. 25. 26. **Mt. 5.** 13-47. **L. 6.** 34. 35. 36.

to **Mt. 6.** 1-34. 7. 1. **L. 6.** 38. **Mt. 7.** 3-20. 12. 35. 36. 37. **7.** 24-29.

[15] the Sermon on the Mount.

Mt. 8. 1. **Mk. 6.** 6. **Mt. 11.** 28. 29. 30. exhorts.

---

*The numbers indicate the leaves in Jefferson's compilation. In the English text, as printed in this edition, they are shown in brackets on the inner margin.

34

36

THE LIFE AND MORALS OF
Jesus of Nazareth

[1]   And it came to pass in those days, that there   **L. 2/1**
went out a decree from Caesar Augustus,
that all the world should be taxed.
(And this taxing was first made when Cyrenius   **2**
was governor of Syria.)
And all went to be taxed, every one into his   **3**
own city.
And Joseph also went up from Galilee, out of   **4**
the city of Nazareth, into Judaea unto the city
of David, which is called Bethlehem (because he
was of the house and lineage of David,)
To be taxed with Mary his espoused wife, being   **5**
great with child.
And so it was, that, while they were there, the   **6**
days were accomplished that she should be delivered.
And she brought forth her first-born son, and   **7**
wrapped him in swaddling clothes, and laid him
in a manger; because there was no room for
them in the inn.
And when eight days were accomplished for the   **21**
circumcising of the child, his name was called
JESUS,

37

L. 2/39   And when they had performed all things according to the law of the Lord, they returned
into Galilee, to their own city Nazareth.

40   And the child grew, and waxed strong in spirit,
filled with wisdom:

42   And when he was twelve years old, they went
up to Jerusalem, after the custom of the feast.

43   And when they had fulfilled the days, as they
returned, the child Jesus tarried behind in
Jerusalem; and Joseph and his mother knew
not of it.

44   But they, supposing him to have been in the
company, went a day's journey; and they sought
him among their kinsfolk and acquaintance.

45   And when they found him not, they turned
back again to Jerusalem, seeking him.

46   And it came to pass, that after three days they [2]
found him in the temple, sitting in the midst
of the doctors, both hearing them, and asking
them questions.

47   And all that heard him were astonished at his
understanding and answers.

48   And when they saw him, they were amazed:
and his mother said unto him, Son, why hast
thou thus dealt with us? behold, thy father and
I have sought thee sorrowing.

51   And he went down with them, and came to
Nazareth, and was subject unto them:

52   And Jesus increased in wisdom and stature.

Now in the fifteenth year of the reign of **L. 3/1**
Tiberius Caesar, Pontius Pilate being
governor of Judaea, and Herod being
tetrarch of Galilee, and his brother Philip tetrarch of Ituraea and of the region of Tracho-
nitis, and Lysanias the tetrarch of Abilene,

Annas and Caiaphas being the high priests, **2**

John did baptize in the wilderness, **Mk. 1/4**

And the same John had his raiment of camel's **Mt. 3/4**
hair, and a leathern girdle about his loins; and
his meat was locusts and wild honey.

Then went out to him Jerusalem, and all Judaea, **5**
and all the region round about Jordan,

And were baptized of him in Jordan. **6**

Then cometh Jesus from Galilee to Jordan unto **Mt. 3/13**
John, to be baptized of him.

And Jesus himself began to be about thirty **L. 3/23**
years of age,

After this he went down to Capernaum, he, and **J. 2/12**
his mother, and his brethren, and his disciples:
and they continued there not many days.

3] And the Jews' passover was at hand, and Jesus **13**
went up to Jerusalem,

And found in the temple those that sold oxen **14**
and sheep and doves, and the changers of money
sitting:

And when he had made a scourge of small **15**
cords, he drove them all out of the temple, and
the sheep and the oxen; and poured out the

J. 2/15 changers' money, and overthrew the tables;

16 And said unto them that sold doves, Take these things hence; make not my Father's house an house of merchandise.

J. 3/22 After these things came Jesus and his disciples into the land of Judaea; and there he tarried with them, and baptized.

Mt. 4/12 Now when Jesus had heard that John was cast into prison, he departed into Galilee;

Mk. 6/17 For Herod himself had sent forth and laid hold upon John, and bound him in prison for Herodias' sake, his brother Philip's wife: for he had married her.

18 For John had said unto Herod, It is not lawful for thee to have thy brother's wife.

19 Therefore Herodias had a quarrel against him, and would have killed him; but she could not:

20 For Herod feared John, knowing that he was a just man and an holy, and observed him; and when he heard him, he did many things, and heard him gladly.

21 And when a convenient day was come, that Herod on his birthday made a supper to his lords, high captains, and chief estates of Galilee;

22 And when the daughter of the said Herodias came in, and danced, and pleased Herod and them that sat with him, the king said unto the damsel, Ask of me whatsoever thou wilt and I will give it thee.

And he sware unto her, Whatsoever thou shalt ask of me, I will give it thee, unto half of my kingdom. **Mk. 6/23**

[4] And she went forth, and said unto her mother, What shall I ask? and she said, The head of John the Baptist. **24**

And she came in straightway with haste unto the king, and asked, saying, I will that thou give me, by and by in a charger, the head of John the Baptist. **25**

And the king was exceedingly sorry; yet for his oath's sake, and for their sakes which sat with him, he would not reject her. **26**

And immediately the king sent an executioner, and commanded his head to be brought: and he went and beheaded him in prison; **27**

And brought his head in a charger, and gave it to the damsel: and the damsel gave it to her mother. **28**

And they went into Capernaum; and straightway on the sabbath day he entered into the synagogue, and taught. **Mk. 1/21**

And they were astonished at his doctrine: for he taught them as one that had authority, and not as the scribes. **22**

At that time Jesus went on the sabbath day through the corn, and his disciples were an hungered, and began to pluck the ears of corn, and to eat. **Mt. 12/1**

41

Mt. 12/2　But when the Pharisees saw it, they said unto him, Behold, thy disciples do that which is not lawful to do upon the sabbath day.

3　But he said unto them, Have ye not read what David did, when he was an hungered, and they that were with him;

4　How he entered into the house of God, and did eat the shewbread, which was not lawful for him to eat, neither for them which were with him, but only for the priests?

5　Or have ye not read in the law, how that on the sabbath days the priests in the temple profane the sabbath, and are blameless?

9　And when he was departed thence, he went into [5 their synagogue:

10　And, behold, there was a man which had his hand withered. And they asked him, saying, Is it lawful to heal on the sabbath days? that they might accuse him.

11　And he said unto them, What man shall there be among you, that shall have one sheep, and if it fall into a pit on the sabbath day, will he not lay hold on it, and lift it out?

12　How much then is a man better than a sheep? Wherefore it is lawful to do well on the sabbath days.

Mk. 2/27　And he said unto them, The sabbath was made for man, and not man for the sabbath:

Mt. 12/14　Then the Pharisees went out, and held a council

42

against him, how they might destroy him.   Mt. 12/14

But when Jesus knew it, he withdrew himself 15
from thence: and great multitudes followed him.

And it came to pass in those days that he went L. 6/12
out* into a mountain to pray, and continued all
night in prayer to God.

And when it was day, he called unto him his 13
disciples: and of them he chose twelve, whom
also he named apostles;

Simon (whom he also named Peter), and Andrew 14
his brother, James and John, Philip and Barthol-
omew,

Matthew and Thomas, James the son of Al- 15
phaeus, and Simon called Zelotes,

And Judas the brother of James, and Judas Isca- 16
riot, which also was the traitor.

And he came down with them, and stood in 17
the plain, and the company of his disciples, and
a great multitude of people out of all Judaea
and Jerusalem, and from the sea coast of Tyre
and Sidon, which came to hear him,

And seeing the multitudes, he went up into Mt. 5/1
a mountain: and when he was set, his disciples came unto him:

And he opened his mouth, and taught them, 2
saying,

Blessed are the poor in spirit: for theirs is the 3
kingdom of heaven.

*Mr. Jefferson changed the word "out" to "up."

Mt. 5/4 Blessed are they that mourn: for they shall be comforted.

5 Blessed are the meek: for they shall inherit the earth.

6 Blessed are they which do hunger and thirst after righteousness: for they shall be filled.

7 Blessed are the merciful: for they shall obtain mercy.

8 Blessed are the pure in heart: for they shall see God.

9 Blessed are the peacemakers: for they shall be called the children of God.

10 Blessed are they which are persecuted for righteousness' sake: for theirs is the kingdom of heaven.

11 Blessed are ye when men shall revile you, and persecute you, and shall say all manner of evil against you falsely, for my sake.

12 Rejoice, and be exceeding glad: for great is your reward in heaven: for so persecuted they the prophets which were before you.

L. 6/24 But woe unto you that are rich! for ye have received your consolation.

25 Woe unto you that are full! for ye shall hunger. Woe unto you that laugh now! for ye shall mourn and weep.

26 Woe unto you, when all men shall speak well of you! for so did their fathers to the false prophets.

Ye are the salt of the earth: but if the salt have **Mt. 5/13** lost his savour, wherewith shall it be salted? it is thenceforth good for nothing, but to be cast out, and to be trodden under foot of men.

Ye are the light of the world. A city that is set **14** on an hill cannot be hid.

7] Neither do men light a candle, and put it under **15** a bushel, but on a candlestick; and it giveth light unto all that are in the house.

Let your light so shine before men, that they **16** may see your good works, and glorify your Father which is in heaven.

Think not that I am come to destroy the law, **17** or the prophets: I am not come to destroy, but to fulfil.

For verily I say unto you, Till heaven and earth **18** pass, one jot or one tittle shall in no wise pass from the law, till all be fulfilled.

Whosoever therefore shall break one of these **19** least commandments, and shall teach men so, he shall be called the least in the kingdom of heaven: but whosoever shall do and teach them, the same shall be called great in the kingdom of heaven.

For I say unto you, That except your right- **20** eousness shall exceed the righteousness of the scribes and Pharisees, ye shall in no case enter into the kingdom of heaven.

Ye have heard that it was said by them of old **21**

Mt. 5/21 time, Thou shall not kill, and whosoever shall kill shall be in danger of the judgment:

22 But I say unto you, That whosoever is angry with his brother without a cause shall be in danger of the judgment: and whosoever shall say to his brother, Raca, shall be in danger of the council: but whosoever shall say, Thou fool, shall be in danger of hell fire.

23 Therefore if thou bring thy gift to the altar, and there rememberest that thy brother hath aught against thee;

24 Leave there thy gift before the altar, and go thy way; first be reconciled to thy brother, and then come and offer thy gift.

25 Agree with thine adversary quickly, whilst thou [are in the way with him; lest at any time the adversary deliver thee to the judge, and the judge deliver thee to the officer, and thou be cast into prison.

26 Verily I say unto thee, Thou shalt by no means come out thence, till thou hast paid the uttermost farthing.

27 Ye have heard that it was said by them of old time, Thou shalt not commit adultery:

28 But I say unto you, That whosoever looketh on a woman to lust after her hath committed adultery with her already in his heart.

29 And if thy right eye offend thee, pluck it out, and cast it from thee: for it is profitable for thee

that one of thy members should perish, and not **Mt. 5/29**
that thy whole body should be cast into hell.

And if thy right hand offend thee, cut it off, **30**
and cast it from thee: for it is profitable for thee
that one of thy members should perish, and not
that thy whole body should be cast into hell.

It hath been said, Whosoever shall put away his **31**
wife, let him give her a writing of divorcement:

But I say unto you, That whosoever shall put **32**
away his wife, saving for the cause of fornication, causeth her to commit adultery: and
whosoever shall marry her that is divorced committeth adultery.

Again, ye have heard that it hath been said **33**
by them of old time, Thou shalt not forswear
thyself, but shalt perform unto the Lord thine
oaths:

But I say unto you, Swear not at all; neither **34**
by heaven; for it is God's throne:

Nor by the earth; for it is his footstool: neither **35**
by Jerusalem; for it is the city of the great King.

Neither shalt thou swear by thy head, because **36**
thou canst not make one hair white or black.

But let your communication be, Yea, yea; Nay, **37**
nay; for whatsoever is more than these cometh
of evil.

Ye have heard that it hath been said, An eye **38**
for an eye, and a tooth for a tooth:

But I say unto you, That ye resist not evil: but **39**

Mt. 5/39 whosoever shall smite thee on thy right cheek, turn to him the other also.

40 And if any man will sue thee at the law, and take away thy coat, let him have thy cloak also.

41 And whosoever shall compel thee to go a mile, go with him twain.

42 Give to him that asketh thee, and from him that would borrow of thee turn not thou away.

43 Ye have heard that it hath been said, Thou shalt love thy neighbour, and hate thine enemy.

44 But I say unto you, Love your enemies, bless them that curse you, do good to them that hate you, and pray for them which despitefully use you, and persecute you;

45 That ye may be the children of your Father which is in heaven: for he maketh his sun to rise on the evil and on the good, and sendeth rain on the just and on the unjust.

46 For if ye love them which love you, what reward have ye? do not even the publicans the same?

47 And if ye salute your brethren only, what do you more than others? do not even the publicans so?

L. 6/34 And if ye lend to them of whom ye hope to receive, what thank have ye? for sinners also lend to sinners, to receive as much again.

35 But love ye your enemies, and do good, and lend, hoping for nothing again; and your reward shall be great, and ye shall be the children

of the Highest: for he is kind unto the unthank- **L. 6/35**
ful and to the evil.

Be ye therefore merciful, as your Father also is **36**
merciful.

Take heed that ye do not your alms before **Mt. 6/1**
men, to be seen of them: otherwise ye
have no reward of your Father which is
in heaven.

Therefore when thou doest thine alms, do not **2**
sound a trumpet before thee, as the hypocrites
do in the synagogues and in the streets, that
they may have glory of men. Verily I say unto
you, They have their reward.

But when thou doest alms, let not thy left hand **3**
know what thy right hand doeth:

That thine alms may be in secret: and thy **4**
Father which seeth in secret himself shall reward thee openly.

And when thou prayest, thou shalt not be as **5**
the hypocrites are: for they love to pray standing in the synagogues and in the corners of the
streets, that they may be seen of men. Verily I
say unto you, They have their reward.

But thou, when thou prayest, enter into thy **6**
closet, and when thou hast shut thy door, pray
to thy Father which is in secret; and thy Father
which seeth in secret shall reward thee openly.

But when ye pray, use not vain repetitions as **7**
the heathen do: for they think that they shall

49

Mt. 6/7 be heard for their much speaking.

8 Be not ye therefore like unto them: for your Father knoweth what things ye have need of, before ye ask him.

9 After this manner therefore pray ye: Our Father [1 which art in heaven, Hallowed be thy name.

10 Thy kingdom come. Thy will be done in earth, as it is in heaven.

11 Give us this day our daily bread.

12 And forgive us our debts, as we forgive our debtors.

13 And lead us not into temptation, but deliver us from evil: For thine is the kingdom, and the power, and the glory, for ever. Amen.

14 For if ye forgive men their trespasses, your heavenly Father will also forgive you:

15 But if ye forgive not men their trespasses, neither will your Father forgive your trespasses.

16 Moreover, when ye fast, be not, as the hypocrites, of a sad countenance: for they disfigure their faces, that they may appear unto men to fast. Verily I say unto you, They have their reward.

17 But thou, when thou fastest, anoint thine head, and wash thy face;

18 That thou appear not unto men to fast, but unto thy Father which is in secret: and thy Father, which seeth in secret, shall reward thee openly.

19 Lay not up for yourselves treasures upon earth,

where moth and rust doth corrupt, and where **Mt. 6/19**
thieves break through and steal:

But lay up for yourselves treasures in heaven, **20**
where neither moth nor rust doth corrupt, and
where thieves do not break through nor steal:

For where your treasure is, there will your heart **21**
be also.

The light of the body is the eye: if therefore **22**
thine eye be single, thy whole body shall be full
of light.

But if thine eye be evil, thy whole body shall **23**
be full of darkness. If therefore the light that is
in thee be darkness, how great is that darkness!

No man can serve two masters: for either he **24**
will hate the one, and love the other; or else he
will hold to the one, and despise the other. Ye
cannot serve God and mammon.

Therefore I say unto you, Take no thought for **25**
your life, what ye shall eat, or what ye shall
drink; nor yet for your body, what ye shall put
on. Is not the life more than meat, and the body
than raiment?

Behold the fowls of the air: for they sow not, **26**
neither do they reap, nor gather into barns; yet
your heavenly Father feedeth them. Are ye not
much better than they?

Which of you by taking thought can add one **27**
cubit unto his stature?

And why take ye thought for raiment? Con- **28**

Mt. 6/28 sider the lilies of the field, how they grow; they toil not, neither do they spin:

29 And yet I say unto you, That even Solomon in all his glory was not arrayed like one of these.

30 Wherefore, if God so clothe the grass of the field, which today is, and tomorrow is cast into the oven, shall he not much more clothe you, O ye of little faith?

31 Therefore, take no thought, saying, What shall we eat? or, What shall we drink? or, Wherewithal shall we be clothed?

32 (For after all these things do the Gentiles seek:) for your heavenly Father knoweth that ye have need of all these things.

33 But seek ye first the kingdom of God, and his righteousness; and all these things shall be added unto you.

34 Take therefore no thought for the morrow: for the morrow shall take thought for the things of itself. Sufficient unto the day is the evil thereof.

Mt. 7/1 Judge not, that ye be not judged.

2 For with what judgment ye judge, ye shall be judged: and with what measure ye mete, it shall be measured to you again.

L. 6/38 Give, and it shall be given unto you; good measure, pressed down, and shaken together, and running over, shall men give into your bosom.

And why beholdest thou the mote that is in thy **Mt. 7/3** brother's eye, but considerest not the beam that is in thine own eye?

Or how wilt thou say to thy brother, Let me **4** pull out the mote out of thine eye; and, behold, a beam is in thine own eye?

Thou hypocrite, first cast out the beam out of **5** thine own eye; and then shalt thou see clearly to cast out the mote out of thy brother's eye.

Give not that which is holy unto the dogs, **6** neither cast ye your pearls before swine, lest they trample them under their feet, and turn again and rend you.

Ask, and it shall be given you; seek, and ye **7** shall find; knock, and it shall be opened unto you:

For every one that asketh receiveth; and he **8** that seeketh findeth; and to him that knocketh it shall be opened.

Or what man is there of you, whom if his son **9** ask bread, will he give him a stone?

Or if he ask a fish, will he give him a serpent? **10**

If ye then, being evil, know how to give good **11** gifts unto your children, how much more shall your Father, which is in heaven, give good things to them that ask him?

Therefore all things whatsoever ye would that **12** men should do to you, do ye even so to them: for this is the law and the prophets.

Mt. 7/13 Enter ye in at the strait gate: for wide is the [1
gate, and broad is the way, that leadeth to de-
struction, and many there be which go in there-
at:

14 Because strait is the gate, and narrow is the
way, which leadeth unto life, and few there be
that find it.

15 Beware of false prophets, which come to you in
sheep's clothing, but inwardly they are ravening wolves.

16 Ye shall know them by their fruits. Do men
gather grapes of thorns, or figs of thistles?

17 Even so every good tree bringeth forth good
fruit; but a corrupt tree bringeth forth evil
fruit.

18 A good tree cannot bring forth evil fruit,
neither can a corrupt tree bring forth good
fruit.

19 Every tree that bringeth not forth good fruit
is hewn down, and cast into the fire.

20 Wherefore by their fruits ye shall know them.

Mt. 12/35 A good man out of the good treasure of the
heart bringeth forth good things: and an evil
man out of the evil treasure bringeth forth evil
things.

36 But I say unto you, That every idle word that
men shall speak, they shall give account thereof
in the day of judgment.

37 For by thy words thou shalt be justified, and by

thy words thou shalt be condemned. **Mt. 12/37**

Therefore whosoever heareth these sayings of **Mt. 7/24**
mine, and doeth them, I will liken him unto a
wise man, which built his house upon a rock:

And the rain descended, and the floods came, **25**
and the winds blew, and beat upon that house;
and it fell not; for it was founded upon a rock.

;] And every one that heareth these sayings of **26**
mine, and doeth them not, shall be likened unto
a foolish man, which built his house upon the
sand:

And the rain descended, and the floods came, **27**
and the winds blew, and beat upon that house;
and it fell; and great was the fall of it.

And it came to pass, when Jesus had ended **28**
these sayings, the people were astonished at his
doctrine.

For he taught them as one having authority, **29**
and not as the scribes.

When he was come down from the moun- **Mt. 8/1**
tain, great multitudes followed him.
And he went round about the villages, **Mk. 6/6**
teaching.

Come unto me, all ye that labour and are heavy **Mt. 11/28**
laden, and I will give you rest.

Take my yoke upon you, and learn of me; for I **29**
am meek and lowly in heart: and ye shall find
rest unto your souls.

For my yoke is easy, and my burden is light. **30**

L. 7/36 And one of the Pharisees desired him that he would eat with him. And he went into the Pharisee's house, and sat down to meat.

37 And, behold, a woman in the city, which was a sinner, when she knew that Jesus sat at meat in the Pharisee's house, brought an alabaster box of ointment.

38 And stood at his feet behind him weeping, and began to wash his feet with tears, and did wipe them with the hairs of her head, and kissed his feet, and anointed them with the ointment.

39 Now when the Pharisee which had bidden him [saw it, he spake within himself, saying, This man, if he were a prophet, would have known who and what manner of woman this is that toucheth him: for she is a sinner.

40 And Jesus answering said unto him, Simon, I have somewhat to say unto thee. And he saith, Master, say on.

41 There was a certain creditor which had two debtors: the one owed five hundred pence, and the other fifty.

42 And when they had nothing to pay, he frankly forgave them both. Tell me therefore, which of them will love him most?

43 Simon answered and said, I suppose that he, to whom he forgave most. And he said unto him, Thou hast rightly judged.

44 And he turned to the woman, and said unto

Simon, Seest thou this woman? I entered into **L. 7/44**
thine house, thou gavest me no water for my
feet: but she hath washed my feet with tears,
and wiped them with the hairs of her head.

Thou gavest me no kiss: but this woman since **45**
the time I came in hath not ceased to kiss my
feet.

My head with oil thou didst not anoint: but **46**
this woman hath anointed my feet with ointment.

There came then his brethren and his mother, **Mk. 3/31**
and, standing without, sent unto him, calling
him.

And the multitude sat about him, and they said **32**
unto him, Behold, thy mother and thy brethren
without seek for thee.

And he answered them, saying, Who is my **33**
mother, or my brethren?

And he looked round about on them which sat **34**
about him, and said, Behold my mother and my
brethren!

For whosoever shall do the will of God, the **35**
same is my brother, and my sister, and mother.

In the mean time, when there were gathered **L. 12/1**
together an innumerable multitude of peo-
ple, insomuch that they trode one upon another, he began to say unto his disciples first of
all, Beware ye of the leaven of the Pharisees,
which is hypocrisy.

L. 12/2 For there is nothing covered, that shall not be revealed; neither hid, that shall not be known.

3 Therefore whatsoever ye have spoken in darkness shall be heard in the light; and that which ye have spoken in the ear in closets shall be proclaimed upon the housetops.

4 And I say unto you my friends, Be not afraid of them that kill the body, and after that have no more that they can do.

5 But I will forewarn you whom ye shall fear: Fear him, which after he hath killed hath power to cast into hell; yea, I say unto you, Fear him.

6 Are not five sparrows sold for two farthings, and not one of them is forgotten before God?

7 But even the very hairs of your head are all numbered. Fear not therefore: ye are of more value than many sparrows.

13 And one of the company said unto him, Master, speak to my brother, that he divide the inheritance with me.

14 And he said unto him, Man, who made me a judge or a divider over you?

15 And he said unto them, Take heed, and beware of covetousness: for a man's life consisteth not in the abundance of things which he possesseth.

16 And he spake a parable unto them, saying, The ground of a certain rich man brought forth plentifully:

17 And he thought within himself, saying, What

shall I do, because I have no room where to be- L. 12/17
stow my fruits?

And he said, This will I do: I will pull down my 18
barns, and build greater; and there will I be-
stow all my fruits and my goods.

And I will say to my soul, Soul, thou hast much 19
goods laid up for many years; take thine ease,
eat, drink, and be merry.

But God said unto him, Thou fool, this night 20
thy soul shall be required of thee: then whose
shall those things be, which thou hast pro-
vided?

So is he that layeth up treasure for himself, and 21
is not rich toward God.

And he said unto his disciples, Therefore I say 22
unto you, Take no thought for your life, what
ye shall eat; neither for the body, what ye shall
put on.

The life is more than meat, and the body is 23
more than raiment.

Consider the ravens: for they neither sow nor 24
reap; which neither have storehouse nor barn;
and God feedeth them: how much more are ye
better than the fowls?

And which of you with taking thought can add 25
to his stature one cubit?

If ye then be not able to do that thing which 26
is least, why take ye thought for the rest?

Consider the lilies how they grow: they toil 27

L. 12/27 not, they spin not; and yet I say unto you, that Solomon in all his glory was not arrayed like one of these.

28 If then God so clothe the grass, which is today in the field, and tomorrow is cast into the oven; how much more will he clothe you, O ye of little faith?

29 And seek not ye what ye shall eat, or what ye shall drink, neither be ye of doubtful mind.

30 For all these things do the nations of the world seek after: and your Father knoweth that ye have need of these things.

31 But rather seek ye the kingdom of God; and all [these things shall be added unto you.

32 Fear not, little flock; for it is your Father's good pleasure to give you the kingdom.

33 Sell that ye have, and give alms; provide yourselves bags which wax not old, a treasure in the heavens that faileth not, where no thief approacheth, neither moth corrupteth.

34 For where your treasure is, there will your heart be also.

35 Let your loins be girded about, and your lights burning;

36 And ye yourselves like unto men that wait for their lord, when he will return from the wedding; that when he cometh and knocketh, they may open unto him immediately.

37 Blessed are those servants, whom the lord when

he cometh shall find watching: verily I say unto **L. 12/37** you, that he shall gird himself, and make them to sit down to meat, and will come forth and serve them.

And if he shall come in the second watch, or **38** come in the third watch, and find them so, blessed are those servants.

And this know, that if the goodman of the **39** house had known what hour the thief would come, he would have watched, and not have suffered his house to be broken through.

Be ye therefore ready also: for the Son of Man **40** cometh at an hour when ye think not.

Then Peter said unto him, Lord, speakest thou **41** this parable unto us, or even to all?

And the Lord said, Who then is that faithful **42** and wise steward, whom his lord shall make ruler over his household, to give them their portion of meat in due season?

Blessed is that servant, whom his lord when he **43** cometh shall find so doing.

Of a truth I say unto you, that he will make **44** him ruler over all that he hath.

But, and if that servant say in his heart, My lord **45** delayeth his coming; and shall begin to beat the menservants and maidens, and to eat and drink, and to be drunken;

The lord of that servant will come in a day **46** when he looketh not for him, and at an hour

L. 12/46 when he is not aware, and will cut him in sunder,

47 And that servant, which knew his lord's will, and prepared not himself, neither did according to his will, shall be beaten with many stripes.

48 But he that knew not and did commit things worthy of stripes, shall be beaten with few stripes. For unto whomsoever much is given, of him shall be much required: and to whom men have committed much, of him they will ask the more.

54 And he said also to the people, When ye see a cloud rise out of the west, straightway ye say, There cometh a shower; and so it is.

55 And when ye see the south wind blow, ye say, There will be heat; and it cometh to pass.

56 Ye hypocrites! ye can discern the face of the sky and of the earth; but how is it that ye do not discern this time?

57 Yea, and why even of yourselves judge ye not what is right?

58 When thou goest with thine adversary to the magistrate, as thou art in the way, give diligence that thou mayest be delivered from him; lest he hale thee to the judge, and the judge deliver thee to the officer, and the officer cast thee into prison.

59 I tell thee, thou shalt not depart thence, till thou hast paid the very last mite.

62

21] There were present at that season some **L. 13/1**
that told him of the Galilaeans, whose
blood Pilate had mingled with their sacrifices.

And Jesus answering said unto them, Suppose **2**
ye that these Galilaeans were sinners above all
the Galilaeans, because they suffered such
things?

I tell you, Nay: but, except ye repent, ye shall **3**
all likewise perish.

Or those eighteen, upon whom the tower in **4**
Siloam fell, and slew them, think ye that they
were sinners above all men that dwelt in Jerusalem?

I tell you, Nay: but, except ye repent, ye shall **5**
all likewise perish.

He spake also this parable; A certain man had **6**
a fig tree planted in his vineyard; and he came
and sought fruit thereon, and found none.

Then he said unto the dresser of his vineyard, **7**
Behold, these three years I come seeking fruit
on this fig tree, and find none: cut it down; why
cumbereth it the ground?

And he answering said unto him, Lord, let it **8**
alone this year also, till I shall dig about it, and
dung it:

And if it bear fruit, well: and if not, then after **9**
that thou shalt cut it down.

And as he spake, a certain Pharisee besought **L. 11/37**

L. 11/37 him to dine with him: and he went in, and sat down to meat.

38 And when the Pharisee saw it, he marvelled that he had not first washed before dinner.

39 And the Lord said unto him, Now do ye Pharisees make clean the outside of the cup and the platter; but your inward part is full of ravening and wickedness.

40 Ye fools! did not he that made which is without make that which is within also?

41 But rather give alms of such things as ye have; and, behold, all things are clean unto you.

42 But woe unto you, Pharisees! for ye tithe mint [2 and rue and all manner of herbs, and pass over judgment and the love of God: these ought ye to have done, and not to leave the other undone.

43 Woe unto you, Pharisees! for ye love the uppermost seats in the synagogues, and greetings in the markets.

44 Woe unto you, scribes and Pharisees, hypocrites! for ye are as graves which appear not, and the men that walk over them are not aware of them.

45 Then answered one of the lawyers, and said unto him, Master, thus saying thou reproachest us also.

46 And he said, Woe unto you also, ye lawyers! for ye lade men with burdens grievous to be

borne, and ye yourselves touch not the burdens **L. 11/46**
with one of your fingers.

Woe unto you, lawyers! for ye have taken away **52**
the key of knowledge: ye entered not in yourselves, and them that were entering in ye hin-
dered.

And as he said these things unto them, the **53**
scribes and the Pharisees began to urge him
vehemently, and to provoke him to speak of
many things:

Laying wait for him, and seeking to catch some- **54**
thing out of his mouth, that they might accuse
him.

The same day went Jesus out of the house, **Mt. 13/1**
and sat by the sea side.
And great multitudes were gathered to- **2**
gether unto him, so that he went into a ship,
and sat; and the whole multitude stood on the
shore.

And he spake many things unto them in para- **3**
bles, saying, Behold, a sower went forth to sow;

And when he sowed, some seeds fell by the way **4**
side, and the fowls came and devoured them:

] Some fell upon stony places, where they had **5**
not much earth: and forthwith they sprung up,
because they had no deepness of earth:

And when the sun was up, they were scorched; **6**
and because they had not root, they withered
away.

Mt. 13/7 And some fell among thorns; and the thorns sprung up, and choked them:

8 But other fell into good ground, and brought forth fruit, some an hundredfold, some sixtyfold, some thirtyfold.

9 Who hath ears to hear, let him hear.

Mk. 4/10 And when he was alone, they that were about him with the twelve asked of him the parable.

Mt. 13/18 Hear ye therefore the parable of the sower.

19 When any one heareth the word of the kingdom, and understandeth it not, then cometh the wicked one, and catcheth away that which was sown in his heart. This is he which received seed by the way side.

20 But he that received the seed into stony places, the same is he that heareth the word, and anon with joy receiveth it;

21 Yet hath he not root in himself, but dureth for a while; for when tribulation or persecution ariseth because of the word, by and by he is offended.

22 He also that received seed among the thorns is he that heareth the word; and the care of this world, and the deceitfulness of riches, choke the word, and he becometh unfruitful.

23 But he that received seed into the good ground is he that heareth the word, and understandeth it; which also beareth fruit, and bringeth forth, some an hundredfold, some sixty, some thirty.

24] And he said unto them, Is a candle brought to **Mk. 4/21**
be put under a bushel, or under a bed? and not
to be set on a candlestick?

For there is nothing hid, which shall not be **22**
manifested; neither was anything kept secret,
but that it should come abroad.

If any man have ears to hear, let him hear. **23**

Another parable put he forth unto them, say- **Mt. 13/24**
ing, The kingdom of heaven is likened unto a
man which sowed good seed in his field:

But while men slept, his enemy came and sowed **25**
tares among the wheat, and went his way.

But when the blade was sprung up, and brought **26**
forth fruit, then appeared the tares also.

So the servants of the householder came and **27**
said unto him, Sir, didst not thou sow good seed
in thy field? from whence then hath it tares?

He said unto them, An enemy hath done this. **28**
The servants said unto him, Wilt thou then that
we go and gather them up?

But he said, Nay; lest while ye gather up the **29**
tares, ye root up also the wheat with them.

Let both grow together until the harvest: and **30**
in the time of harvest I will say to the reapers,
Gather ye together first the tares, and bind
them in bundles to burn them: but gather the
wheat into my barn.

Then Jesus sent the multitude away, and went **36**
into the house: and his disciples came unto him,

Mt. 13/36 saying, Declare unto us the parable of the tares of the field.

37 He answered and said unto them, He that soweth the good seed is the Son of Man;

38 The field is the world; the good seed are the children of the kingdom; but the tares are the children of the wicked one;

39 The enemy that sowed them is the devil; the [2 harvest is the end of the world; and the reapers are the angels.

40 As therefore the tares are gathered and burned in the fire; so shall it be in the end of this world.

41 The Son of Man shall send forth his angels, and they shall gather out of his kingdom all things that offend, and them which do iniquity;

42 And shall cast them into a furnace of fire; there shall be wailing and gnashing of teeth.

43 Then shall the righteous shine forth as the sun in the kingdom of their Father. Who hath ears to hear, let him hear.

44 Again, the kingdom of heaven is like unto treasure hid in a field; the which when a man hath found, he hideth, and for joy thereof goeth and selleth all that he hath, and buyeth that field.

45 Again, the kingdom of heaven is like unto a merchant man, seeking goodly pearls:

46 Who, when he had found one pearl of great

price, went and sold all that he had, and bought Mt. 13/46
it.

Again, the kingdom of heaven is like unto a 47
net, that was cast into the sea, and gathered of
every kind:

Which, when it was full, they drew to shore, 48
and sat down, and gathered the good into vessels, but cast the bad away.

So shall it be at the end of the world: the angels 49
shall come forth, and sever the wicked from
among the just,

And shall cast them into the furnace of fire; 50
there shall be wailing and gnashing of teeth.

Jesus saith unto them, Have ye understood all 51
these things? They say unto him, Yea, Lord.

Then said he unto them, Therefore every scribe 52
which is instructed unto the kingdom of heaven
is like unto a man that is an householder, which
bringeth forth out of his treasure things new
and old.

And he said, So is the kingdom of God, as if a Mk. 4/26
man should cast seed into the ground;

And should sleep, and rise night and day, and 27
the seed should spring and grow up, he knoweth
not how.

For the earth bringeth forth fruit of herself; 28
first the blade, then the ear, after that the full
corn in the ear.

But when the fruit is brought forth, immediate- 29

Mk. 4/29 ly he putteth in the sickle, because the harvest is come.

30 And he said, Whereunto shall we liken the kingdom of God? or with what comparison shall we compare it?

31 It is like a grain of mustard seed, which, when it is sown in the earth, is less than all the seeds that be in the earth:

32 But when it is sown, it groweth up, and becometh greater than all herbs, and shooteth out great branches; so that the fowls of the air may lodge under the shadow of it.

33 And with many such parables spake he the word unto them, as they were able to hear it.

34 But without a parable spake he not unto them: and when they were alone, he expounded all things to his disciples.

L. 9/57 And it came to pass, that, as they went in the way, a certain man said unto him, Lord, I will follow thee whithersoever thou goest.

58 And Jesus said unto him, Foxes have holes, and birds of the air have nests; but the Son of Man hath not where to lay his head.

59 And he said unto another, Follow me. But he said, Lord, suffer me first to go and bury my father.

60 Jesus said unto him, Let the dead bury their dead: but go thou and preach the kingdom of God.

And another also said, Lord, I will follow thee; **L. 9/61**
but let me first go bid them farewell, which are
at home at my house.

And Jesus said unto him, No man, having put **62**
his hand to the plough, and looking back, is fit
for the kingdom of God.

27] And after these things he went forth, and saw **L. 5/27**
a publican, named Levi, sitting at the receipt of
custom: and he said unto him, Follow me.

And he left all, rose up, and followed him. **28**

And Levi made him a great feast in his own **29**
house: and

Many publicans and sinners sat also together **Mk. 2/15**
with Jesus and his disciples: for there were
many, and they followed him.

And when the scribes and Pharisees saw him eat **16**
with publicans and sinners, they said unto his
disciples, How is it that he eateth and drinketh
with publicans and sinners?

When Jesus heard it, he saith unto them, They **17**
that are whole have no need of the physician,
but they that are sick: I came not to call the
righteous, but sinners to repentance.

And he spake also a parable unto them; No **L. 5/36**
man putteth a piece of a new garment upon an
old; if otherwise, then both the new maketh a
rent, and the piece that was taken out of the
new agreeth not with the old.

And no man putteth new wine into old bottles; **37**

71

L. 5/37 else the new wine will burst the bottles, and be spilled, and the bottles shall perish.

38 But new wine must be put into new bottles; and both are preserved.

Mt. 13/53 And it came to pass, that when Jesus had finished these parables, he departed thence.

54 And when he was come into his own country, he taught them in their synagogue, insomuch that they were astonished, and said, Whence hath this man this wisdom, and these mighty works?

55 Is not this the carpenter's son? is not his mother called Mary? and his brethren, James, and Joses, and Simon, and Judas?

56 And his sisters, are they not all with us? When then hath this man all these things?   [:

57 And they were offended in him. But Jesus said unto them, A prophet is not without honour save in his own country, and in his own house.

Mt. 9/36 But when he saw the multitudes, he was moved with compassion on them, because they fainted, and were scattered abroad, as sheep having no shepherd.

Mk. 6/7 And he called unto him the twelve and began to send them forth by two and two,

Mt. 10/5 And commanded them, saying, Go not into the way of the Gentiles, and into any city of the Samaritans enter ye not:

6 But go rather to the lost sheep of the house of Israel.

Provide neither gold, nor silver, nor brass in **Mt. 10/9**
your purses,

Nor scrip for your journey, neither two coats, **10**
neither shoes, nor yet staves: for the workman
is worthy of his meat.

And into whatsoever city or town ye shall **11**
enter, enquire who in it is worthy; and there
abide till ye go thence.

And when ye come into an house, salute it. **12**

And if the house be worthy, let your peace **13**
come upon it: but if it be not worthy, let your
peace return to you.

And whosoever shall not receive you, nor hear **14**
your words, when ye depart out of that house
or city, shake off the dust of your feet.

Verily I say unto you, it shall be more tolerable **15**
for the land of Sodom and Gomorrha in the
day of judgment, than for that city.

Behold, I send you forth as sheep in the midst **16**
of wolves: be ye therefore wise as serpents, and
harmless as doves.

But beware of men: for they will deliver you up **17**
to the councils, and they will scourge you in
their synagogues;

And ye shall be brought before governors and **18**
kings for my sake, for a testimony against them
and the Gentiles.

But when they persecute you in this city, flee **23**
ye into another:

Mt. 10/26 Fear them not therefore: for there is nothing covered, that shall not be revealed; and hid, that shall not be known.

27 What I tell you in darkness, that speak ye in light: and what ye hear in the ear, that preach ye upon the housetops.

28 And fear not them which kill the body, but are not able to kill the soul: but rather fear him which is able to destroy both soul and body in hell.

29 Are not two sparrows sold for a farthing? and one of them shall not fall on the ground without your Father.

30 But the very hairs of your head are all numbered.

31 Fear ye not therefore, ye are of more value than many sparrows.

Mk. 6/12 And they went out and preached that men should repent.

30 And the apostles gathered themselves together unto Jesus, and told him all things, both what they had done and what they had taught.

J. 7/1 After these things Jesus walked in Galilee: for he would not walk in Jewry, because the Jews sought to kill him.

Mk. 7/1 Then came together unto him the Pharisees, and certain of the scribes, which came from Jerusalem.

2 And when they saw some of his disciples eat

74

bread with defiled (that is to say, with un- **Mk. 7/2**
washen) hands, they found fault.

For the Pharisees, and all the Jews, except they **3**
wash their hands oft, eat not, holding the tradition of the elders.

o] And when they come from the market, except **4**
they wash, they eat not. And many other
things there be, which they have received to
hold, as the washing of cups, and pots, and of
brasen vessels, and tables.

Then the Pharisees and scribes asked him, Why **5**
walk not thy disciples according to the tradition of the elders, but eat bread with unwashen
hands?

And when he had called all the people unto **14**
him he said unto them, Hearken unto me every
one of you, and understand:

There is nothing from without a man, that **15**
entering into him can defile him: but the things
which come out of him, those are they that defile the man.

If any man have ears to hear, let him hear. **16**

And when he was entered into the house from **17**
the people, his disciples asked him concerning
the parable.

And he saith unto them. Are ye so without **18**
understanding also? Do ye not perceive, that
whatsoever thing from without entereth into
the man, it cannot defile him;

Mk. 7/19 Because it entereth not into his heart, but into the belly, and goeth out into the draught, purging all meats?

20 And he said, That which cometh out of the man, that defileth the man.

21 For from within, out of the heart of men, proceed evil thoughts, adulteries, fornications, murders,

22 Thefts, covetousness, wickedness, deceit, lasciviousness, an evil eye, blasphemy, pride, foolishness:

23 All these evil things come from within, and defile the man.

24 And from thence he arose, and went into the borders of Tyre and Sidon, and entered into an house, and would have no man know it: but he could not be hid.

Mt. 18/1 At the same time came the disciples unto [Jesus, saying, Who is the greatest in the kingdom of heaven?

2 And Jesus called a little child unto him, and set him in the midst of them,

3 And said, Verily I say unto you, Except ye be converted, and become as little children, ye shall not enter into the kingdom of heaven.

4 Whosoever therefore shall humble himself as this little child, the same is greatest in the kingdom of heaven.

7 Woe unto the world because of offences! for it

76

must needs be that offences come; but woe to **Mt. 18/7**
that man by whom the offence cometh!

Wherefore if thy hand or thy foot offend thee, **8**
cut them off, and cast them from thee: it is
better for thee to enter into life halt or maimed,
rather than having two hands or two feet to be
cast into everlasting fire.

And if thine eye offend thee, pluck it out, and **9**
cast it from thee: it is better for thee to enter
into life with one eye, rather than having two
eyes to be cast into hell fire.

How think ye? if a man have an hundred sheep, **12**
and one of them be gone astray, doth he not
leave the ninety and nine, and goeth into the
mountains, and seeketh that which is gone
astray?

And if so be that he find it, verily I say unto **13**
you, he rejoiceth more of that sheep, than of
the ninety and nine which went not astray.

Even so it is not the will of your Father which **14**
is in heaven, that one of these little ones should
perish.

Moreover if thy brother shall trespass against **15**
thee, go and tell him his fault between thee
and him alone: if he shall hear thee, thou hast
gained thy brother.

But if he will not hear thee, then take with thee **16**
one or two more, that in the mouth of two or
three witnesses every word may be established.

Mt. 18/17 And if he shall neglect to hear them, tell it unto the church: but if he neglect to hear the church, let him be unto thee as an heathen man and a publican.

21 Then came Peter to him, and said, Lord, how oft shall my brother sin against me, and I forgive him? till seven times?

22 Jesus saith unto him, I say not unto thee, Until seven times: but, Until seventy times seven.

23 Therefore is the kingdom of heaven likened unto a certain king, which would take account of his servants.

24 And when he had begun to reckon, one was brought unto him, which owed him ten thousand talents.

25 But forasmuch as he had not to pay, his lord commanded him to be sold, and his wife, and children, and all that he had, and payment to be made.

26 The servant therefore fell down, and worshipped him, saying, Lord, have patience with me, and I will pay thee all.

27 Then the lord of that servant was moved with compassion, and loosed him, and forgave him the debt.

28 But the same servant went out, and found one of his fellowservants, which owed him an hundred pence: and he laid hands on him, and took him by the throat, saying, Pay me that thou owest.

And his fellowservant fell down at his feet, and **Mt. 18/29**
besought him, saying, have patience with me,
and I will pay thee all.

And he would not: but went and cast him into **30**
prison, till he should pay the debt.

3] So when his fellowservants saw what was done, **31**
they were very sorry, and came and told unto
their lord all that was done.

Then his lord, after that he had called him, said **32**
unto him, O thou wicked servant, I forgave
thee all that debt, because thou desiredst me:
Shouldest not thou also have had compassion **33**
on thy fellowservant, even as I had pity on thee?
And his lord was wroth, and delivered him to **34**
the tormentors, till he should pay all that was
due unto him.

So likewise shall my heavenly Father do also **35**
unto you, if ye from your hearts forgive not
every one his brother their trespasses.

After these things the Lord appointed other **L. 10/1**
seventy also, and sent them two and two
before his face into every city and place,
whither he himself would come.

Therefore said he unto them, The harvest truly **2**
is great, but the labourers are few: pray ye
therefore the Lord of the harvest, that he would
send forth labourers into his harvest.

Go your ways: behold, I send you forth as **3**
lambs among wolves.

L. 10/4 Carry neither purse, nor scrip, nor shoes: and salute no man by the way.

5 And into whatsoever house ye enter, first say, Peace be to this house.

6 And if the son of peace be there, your peace shall rest upon it: if not, it shall turn to you again.

7 And in the same house remain, eating and drinking such things as they give: for the labourer is worthy of his hire. Go not from house to house.

8 And into whatsoever city ye enter, and they receive you, eat such things as are set before you:

10 But into whatsoever city ye enter, and they receive you not, go your ways out into the streets of the same, and say,

11 Even the very dust of your city, which cleaveth on us, we do wipe off against you: notwithstanding be ye sure of this, that the kingdom of God is come nigh unto you.

12 But I say unto you that it shall be more tolerable in that day for Sodom, than for that city.

J. 7/2 Now the Jews' feast of tabernacles was at hand.

3 His brethren therefore said unto him, Depart hence, and go into Judaea, that thy disciples also may see the works that thou doest.

4 For there is no man that doeth any thing in secret, and he himself seeketh to be known openly. If thou do these things, shew thyself to the world.

80

For neither did his brethren believe in him. **J. 7/5**

Then Jesus said unto them, My time is not yet **6**
come: but your time is alway ready.

The world cannot hate you; but me it hateth, **7**
because I testify of it, that the works thereof
are evil.

Go ye up unto this feast: I go not up yet unto **8**
this feast; for my time is not yet full come.

When he had said these words unto them, he **9**
abode still in Galilee.

But when his brethren were gone up, then went **10**
he also up unto the feast, not openly, but as it
were in secret.

Then the Jews sought him at the feast, and said, **11**
Where is he?

And there was much murmuring among the **12**
people concerning him: for some said, He is a
good man; others said, Nay; but he deceiveth
the people.

Howbeit no man spake openly of him for fear **13**
of the Jews.

Now about the midst of the feast Jesus went up **14**
into the temple, and taught.

And the Jews marvelled, saying, How knoweth **15**
this man letters, having never learned?

Jesus answered them, and said, **16**

Did not Moses give you the law, and yet none **19**
of you keepeth the law? Why go ye about to
kill me?

J. 7/20 The people answered and said, Thou hast a devil: who goeth about to kill thee?

21 Jesus answered and said unto them, I have done one work, and ye all marvel.

22 Moses therefore gave unto you circumcision, (not because it is of Moses but of the fathers,) and ye on the sabbath day circumcise a man.

23 If a man on the sabbath day receive circumcision, that the law of Moses should not be broken; are ye angry at me, because I have made a man every whit whole on the sabbath day?

24 Judge not according to the appearance, but judge righteous judgment.

25 Then said some of them of Jerusalem, Is not this he, whom they seek to kill?

26 But, lo, he speaketh boldly, and they say nothing unto him. Do the rulers know indeed that this is the very Christ?

32 The Pharisees heard that the people murmured such things concerning him; and the Pharisees and the chief priests sent officers to take him.

43 So there was a division among the people because of him.

44 And some of them would have taken him; but no man laid hands on him.

45 Then came the officers to the chief priests and Pharisees; and they said unto them, Why have ye not brought him?

82

The officers answered, Never man spake like **J. 7/46** this man.

Then answered them the Pharisees, Are ye also **47** deceived?

Have any of the rulers or of the Pharisees be- **48** lieved on him?

But this people who knoweth not the law are **49** cursed.

] Nicodemus saith unto them, (he that came to **50** Jesus by night, being one of them,)

Doth our law judge any man, before it hear **51** him, and know what he doeth?

They answered and said unto him, Art thou **52** also of Galilee? Search, and look: for out of Galilee ariseth no prophet.

And every man went unto his own house. **53**

Jesus went unto the mount of Olives. **J. 8/1**
And early in the morning he came again **2** into the temple, and all the people came unto him; and he sat down, and taught them.

And the scribes and Pharisees brought unto him **3** a woman taken in adultery; and when they had set her in the midst,

They say unto him, Master, this woman was **4** taken in adultery, in the very act.

Now Moses in the law commanded us, that **5** such should be stoned: but what sayest thou?

This they said, tempting him, that they might **6** have to accuse him. But Jesus stooped down,

J. 8/6 and with his finger wrote on the ground, as though he heard them not.

7 So when they continued asking him, he lifted up himself, and said unto them, He that is without sin among you, let him first cast a stone at her.

8 And again he stooped down, and wrote on the ground.

9 And they which heard it, being convicted by their own conscience, went out one by one, beginning at the eldest, even unto the last: and Jesus was left alone, and the woman standing in the midst.

10 When Jesus had lifted up himself, and saw none but the woman, he said unto her, Woman, where are those thine accusers? hath no man condemned thee?

11 She said, No man, Lord. And Jesus said unto her, Neither do I condemn thee: go, and sin no more.

J. 9/1 And as Jesus passed by, he saw a man which was blind from his birth.

2 And his disciples asked him, saying, Master, who did sin, this man, or his parents, that he was born blind?

3 Jesus answered, Neither hath this man sinned, nor his parents: but that the works of God should be made manifest in him.

J. 10/1 Verily, verily, I say unto you, He that entereth not by the door into the sheepfold, but climb

84

eth up some other way, the same is a thief and **J. 10/1**
a robber.

But he that entereth in by the door is the shep- **2**
herd of the sheep.

To him the porter openeth; and the sheep hear **3**
his voice; and he calleth his own sheep by
name, and leadeth them out.

And when he putteth forth his own sheep, he **4**
goeth before them, and his sheep follow him:
for they know his voice.

And a stranger will they not follow, but will **5**
flee from him: for they know not the voice of
strangers.

I am the good shepherd: the good shepherd giv- **11**
eth his life for the sheep.

But he that is an hireling, and not the shepherd, **12**
whose own the sheep are not, seeth the wolf
coming, and leaveth the sheep, and fleeth: and
the wolf catcheth them, and scattereth the
sheep.

The hireling fleeth, because he is an hireling, **13**
and careth not for the sheep.

I am the good shepherd, and know my sheep **14**
and am known of mine.

And other sheep I have, which are not of this **16**
fold: them also I must bring, and they shall hear
my voice; and there shall be one fold, and one
shepherd.

And, behold, a certain lawyer stood up, and **L. 10/25**

L. 10/25 tempted him, saying, Master, what shall I do to inherit eternal life?

26 He said unto him, What is written in the law? how readest thou?

27 And he answering said, Thou shalt love the Lord thy God with all thy heart, and with all thy soul, and with all thy strength, and with all thy mind; and thy neighbour as thyself.

28 And he said unto him, Thou hast answered right: this do, and thou shalt live.

29 But he, willing to justify himself, said unto Jesus, And who is my neighbour?

30 And Jesus answering said, A certain man went down from Jerusalem to Jericho, and fell among thieves, which stripped him of his raiment, and wounded him, and departed, leaving him half dead.

31 And, by chance, there came down a certain priest that way: and when he saw him, he passed by on the other side.

32 And likewise a Levite, when he was at the place, came and looked on him, and passed by on the other side.

33 But a certain Samaritan, as he journeyed, came where he was: and when he saw him, he had compassion on him.

34 And went to him, and bound up his wounds, pouring in oil and wine, and set him on his own

beast, and brought him to an inn, and took care **L. 10/34**
of him.

And on the morrow when he departed, he took **35**
out two pence, and gave them to the host, and
said unto him, Take care of him; and whatsoever thou spendest more, when I come again,
I will repay thee.

Which now of these three, thinkest thou, was **36**
neighbour unto him that fell among the thieves?

And he said, He that shewed mercy on him. **37**
Then said Jesus unto him, Go, and do thou
likewise.

And it came to pass, that, as he was praying **L. 11/1**
in a certain place, when he ceased, one of
his disciples said unto him, Lord, teach
us to pray, as John also taught his disciples.

And he said unto them, When ye pray, say, Our **2**
Father which art in heaven, Hallowed by thy
name. Thy kingdom come. Thy will be done, as
in heaven, so in earth.

Give us day by day our daily bread. **3**

And forgive us our sins; for we also forgive **4**
every one that is indebted to us. And lead us
not into temptation; but deliver us from evil.

And he said unto them, Which of you shall **5**
have a friend, and shall go unto him at midnight, and say unto him, Friend, lend me three
loaves;

L. 11/6 For a friend of mine in his journey is come to me, and I have nothing to set before him?

7 And he from within shall answer and say, Trouble me not; the door is now shut, and my children are with me in bed; I cannot rise and give thee.

8 I say unto you, Though he will not rise and give him, because he is his friend, yet because of his importunity he will rise and give him as many as he needeth.

9 And I say unto you, Ask, and it shall be given you; seek, and ye shall find; knock, and it shall be opened unto you.

10 For every one that asketh receiveth; and he that seeketh findeth; and to him that knocketh it shall be opened.

11 If a son shall ask bread of any of you that is a father, will he give him a stone? or if he ask a fish, will he for a fish give him a serpent?

12 Or if he shall ask an egg, will he offer him a scorpion?

13 If ye then, being evil, know how to give good gifts unto your children: how much more shall your heavenly Father give the Holy Spirit to them that ask him?

L. 14/1 And it came to pass, as he went into the house of one of the chief Pharisees to eat bread on the sabbath day, that they watched him.

And, behold, there was a certain man before **L. 14/2** him which had the dropsy.

And Jesus answering spake unto the lawyers **3** and Pharisees, saying, Is it lawful to heal on the sabbath day?

And they held their peace.   **4**

And he saith unto them,

Which of you shall have an ass or an ox fallen **5** into a pit, and will not straightway pull him out on the sabbath day?

And they could not answer him again to these **6** things.

And he put forth a parable to those which were **7** bidden, when he marked how they chose out the chief rooms; saying unto them,

When thou art bidden of any man to a wedding, **8** sit not down in the highest room; lest a more honourable man than thou be bidden of him;

And he that bade thee and him come and say **9** to thee, Give this man place; and thou begin with shame to take the lowest room.

But when thou art bidden, go and sit down in **10** the lowest room; that when he that bade thee cometh, he may say unto thee, Friend, go up higher: then shalt thou have worship in the presence of them that sit at meat with thee.

For whosoever exalteth himself shall be abased; **11** and he that humbleth himself shall be exalted.

Then said he also to him that bade him, When **12**

L. 14/12   thou makest a dinner or a supper, call not thy friends, nor thy brethren, neither thy kinsmen, nor thy rich neighbours; lest they also bid thee again, and a recompense be made thee.

13   But when thou makest a feast, call the poor, the [4 maimed, the lame, the blind:

14   And thou shalt be blessed; for they cannot recompense thee: for thou shalt be recompensed at the resurrection of the just.

16   Then said he unto him, A certain man made a great supper, and bade many:

17   And sent his servant at supper time to say to them that were bidden, Come; for all things are now ready.

18   And they all with one consent began to make excuse. The first said unto him, I have bought a piece of ground, and I must needs go and see it: I pray thee have me excused.

19   And another said, I have bought five yoke of oxen, and I go to prove them: I pray thee have me excused.

20   And another said, I have married a wife, and therefore I cannot come.

21   So that servant came, and shewed his lord these things. Then the master of the house being angry said to his servant, Go out quickly into the streets and lanes of the city, and bring in hither the poor, and the maimed, and the halt, and the blind.

And the servant said, Lord, it is done as thou **L. 14/22**
hast commanded, and yet there is room.

And the lord said unto the servant, Go out into **23**
the highways and hedges and compel them to
come in, that my house may be filled.

For I say unto you, That none of those men **24**
which were bidden shall taste of my supper.

For which of you, intending to build a tower, **28**
sitteth not down first, and counteth the cost,
whether he have sufficient to finish it?

Lest haply, after he hath laid the foundation, **29**
and is not able to finish it, all that behold it begin to mock him,

Saying, This man began to build, and was not **30**
able to finish.

Or what king, going to make war against an- **31**
other king, sitteth not down first, and consult-
eth whether he be able with ten thousand to
meet him that cometh against him with twenty
thousand?

Or else, while the other is yet a great way off, **32**
he sendeth an ambassage, and desireth condi-
tions of peace.

Then drew near unto him all the publicans **L. 15/1**
and sinners for to hear him.

And the Pharisees and scribes murmured, **2**
saying, This man receiveth sinners, and eateth
with them.

And he spake this parable unto them saying, **3**

L. 15/4 What man of you, having an hundred sheep, if he lose one of them, doth not leave the ninety and nine in the wilderness, and go after that which is lost, until he find it?

5 And when he hath found it, he layeth it on his shoulders, rejoicing.

6 And when he cometh home, he calleth together his friends and neighbours, saying unto them, Rejoice with me; for I have found my sheep which was lost.

7 I say unto you, that likewise joy shall be in heaven over one sinner that repenteth, more than over ninety and nine just persons, which need no repentance.

8 Either what woman having ten pieces of silver, if she lose one piece, doth not light a candle, and sweep the house, and seek diligently till she find it?

9 And when she hath found it, she calleth her friends and her neighbours together; saying, Rejoice with me; for I have found the piece which I had lost.

10 Likewise, I say unto you, there is joy in the presence of the angels of God over one sinner that repenteth.

11 And he said, A certain man had two sons:

12 And the younger of them said to his father, Father, give me the portion of goods that falleth to me. And he divided unto them his living.

And not many days after the younger son gath- L. 15/13
ered all together, and took his journey into a
far country, and there wasted his substance
with riotous living.

And when he had spent all, there arose a mighty 14
famine in that land; and he began to be in want.

And he went and joined himself to a citizen of 15
that country; and he sent him into his fields to
feed swine.

And he would fain have filled his belly with the 16
husks that the swine did eat; and no man gave
unto him.

And when he came to himself, he said, How 17
many hired servants of my father's have bread
enough and to spare, and I perish with hunger!

I will arise and go to my father, and will say 18
unto him, Father, I have sinned against heaven,
and before thee,

And am no more worthy to be called thy son: 19
make me as one of thy hired servants.

And he arose, and came to his father. But when 20
he was yet a great way off, his father saw him,
and had compassion, and ran, and fell on his
neck, and kissed him.

And the son said unto him, Father, I have 21
sinned against heaven, and in thy sight, and am
no more worthy to be called thy son.

But the father said to his servants, Bring forth 22
the best robe, and put it on him; and put a ring

L. 15/22 on his hand, and shoes on his feet:

23 And bring hither the fatted calf, and kill it; and let us eat, and be merry:

24 For this my son was dead, and is alive again; he [44 was lost, and is found. And they began to be merry:

25 Now his elder son was in the field: and as he came and drew nigh to the house, he heard musick and dancing.

26 And he called one of the servants, and asked what these things meant.

27 And he said unto him, Thy brother is come; and thy father hath killed the fatted calf, because he hath received him safe and sound.

28 And he was angry, and would not go in: therefore came his father out, and entreated him.

29 And he answering said to his father, Lo, these many years do I serve thee, neither transgressed I at any time thy commandment: and yet thou never gavest me a kid, that I might make merry with my friends:

30 But as soon as this thy son was come, which hath devoured thy living with harlots, thou hast killed for him the fatted calf.

31 And he said unto him, Son, thou art ever with me, and all that I have is thine.

32 It was meet that we should make merry, and be glad; for this thy brother was dead, and is alive again; and was lost, and is found.

And he said also unto his disciples, There was a certain rich man, which had a steward; and the same was accused unto him that he had wasted his goods. L. 16/1

And he called him, and said unto him, How is it that I hear this of thee? give an account of thy stewardship; for thou mayest be no longer steward. 2

Then the steward said within himself, What shall I do? for my lord taketh away from me the stewardship: I cannot dig; to beg I am ashamed. 3

5| I am resolved what to do, that, when I am put out of the stewardship, they may receive me into their houses. 4

So he called every one of his lord's debtors unto him, and said unto the first, How much owest thou unto my lord? 5

And he said, An hundred measures of oil. And he said unto him, Take thy bill, and sit down quickly, and write fifty. 6

Then saith he to another, And how much owest thou? And he said, An hundred measures of wheat. And he said unto him, Take thy bill, and write fourscore. 7

And the lord commended the unjust steward, because he had done wisely: for the children of this world are in their generation wiser than the children of light. 8

And I say unto you, Make to yourselves friends 9

L. 16/9 of the mammon of unrighteousness; that, when
ye fail, they may receive you into everlasting
habitations.

10 He that is faithful in that which is least is faithful also in much: and he that is unjust in the
least is unjust also in much.

11 If therefore ye have not been faithful in the un-
righteous mammon, who will commit to your
trust the true riches?

12 And if ye have not been faithful in that which
is another man's, who shall give you that which
is your own?

13 No servant can serve two masters: for either
he will hate the one, and love the other; or else
he will hold to the one, and despise the other.
Ye cannot serve God and mammon.

14 And the Pharisees also, who were covetous,
heard all these things: and they derided him.

15 And he said unto them, Ye are they which justify yourselves before men; but God knoweth
your hearts: for that which is highly esteemed
among men is abomination in the sight of God.

18 Whosoever putteth away his wife, and marrieth
another, committeth adultery: and whosoever
marrieth her that is put away from her husband
committeth adultery.

19 There was a certain rich man, which was
clothed in purple and fine linen, and fared
sumptuously every day:

And there was a certain beggar named Lazarus, L. 16/20
which was laid at his gate full of sores,

And desiring to be fed with the crumbs which 21
fell from the rich man's table: moreover the
dogs came and licked his sores.

And it came to pass, that the beggar died, and 22
was carried by the angels into Abraham's bosom: the rich man also died, and was buried;

And in hell he lifted up his eyes, being in tor- 23
ments, and seeth Abraham afar off, and Lazarus
in his bosom.

And he cried, and said, Father Abraham, have 24
mercy on me; and send Lazarus, that he may
dip the tip of his finger in water, and cool my
tongue; for I am tormented in this flame.

But Abraham said, Son, remember that thou in 25
thy lifetime receivedst thy good things, and
likewise Lazarus evil things: but now he is
comforted, and thou art tormented.

And beside all this, between us and you there is 26
a great gulf fixed: so that they which would
pass from hence to you cannot; neither can
they pass to us, that would come from thence.

Then he said, I pray thee therefore, father, that 27
thou wouldest send him to my father's house:

For I have five brethren; that he may testify 28
unto them, lest they also come into this place
of torment.

Abraham saith unto him, They have Moses and 29

L. 16/29 the prophets; let them hear them.

30 And he said, Nay, father Abraham: but if one [47
went unto them from the dead, they will repent.

31 And he said unto him, If they hear not Moses
and the prophets, neither will they be persuaded, though one rose from the dead.

L. 17/1 Then said he unto the disciples, It is impossible but that offences will come: but
woe unto him, through whom they come!

2 It were better for him that a millstone were
hanged about his neck, and he cast into the sea,
than that he should offend one of these little
ones.

3 Take heed to yourselves: If thy brother trespass
against thee, rebuke him; and if he repent, forgive him.

4 And if he trespass against thee seven times in
a day, and seven times in a day turn again to
thee, saying, I repent; thou shalt forgive him.

7 But which of you, having a servant plowing
or feeding cattle, will say unto him by and by,
when he is come from the field, Go and sit down
to meat?

8 And will not rather say unto him, Make ready
wherewith I may sup, and gird thyself, and
serve me, till I have eaten and drunken; and
afterward thou shalt eat and drink?

9 Doth he thank that servant because he did the

things that were commanded him? I trow not. L. 17/9
So likewise ye, when ye shall have done all 10
these things which are commanded you, say,
We are unprofitable servants: we have done
that which was our duty to do.

And when he was demanded of the Pharisees, 20
when the kingdom of God should come, he
answered them and said, The kingdom of God
cometh not with observation:

8] And as it was in the days of Noe, so shall it be 26
also in the days of the Son of Man.

They did eat, they drank, they married wives, 27
they were given in marriage, until the day that
Noe entered into the ark, and the flood came,
and destroyed them all.

Likewise also, as it was in the days of Lot; they 28
did eat, they drank, they bought, they sold,
they planted, they builded;

But the same day that Lot went out of Sodom 29
it rained fire and brimstone from heaven, and
destroyed them all.

Even thus shall it be in the day when the Son 30
of Man is revealed.

In that day, he which shall be upon the house- 31
top, and his stuff in the house, let him not come
down to take it away: and he that is in the field,
let him likewise not return back.

Remember Lot's wife. 32

Whosoever shall seek to save his life shall lose 33

99

L. 17/33 it: and whosoever shall lose his life shall preserve it.

34 I tell you, in that night there shall be two men in one bed; the one shall be taken, and the other shall be left.

35 Two women shall be grinding together; the one shall be taken, and the other left.

37 Two men shall be in the field; the one shall be taken, and the other left.

L. 18/1 And he spake a parable unto them to this end, that men ought always to pray, and not to faint;

2 Saying, There was in a city a judge, which feared not God, neither regarded man:

3 And there was a widow in that city; and she came unto him, saying, Avenge me of mine adversary.

4 And he would not for a while: but afterward he [said within himself, Though I fear not God, nor regard man;

5 Yet because this widow troubleth me, I will avenge her, lest by her continual coming she weary me.

6 And the Lord said, Hear what the unjust judge saith.

7 And shall not God avenge his own elect, which cry day and night unto him, though he bear long with them?

8 I tell you that he will avenge them speedily.

Nevertheless when the Son of Man cometh, **L. 18/8**
shall he find faith on the earth?

And he spake this parable unto certain which **9**
trusted in themselves, that they were righteous,
and despised others:

Two men went up into the temple to pray; the **10**
one a Pharisee, and the other a publican.

The Pharisee stood and prayed thus with him- **11**
self, God, I thank thee, that I am not as other
men are, extortioners, unjust, adulterers, or
even as this publican.

I fast twice in the week, I give tithes of all that **12**
I possess.

And the publican, standing afar off, would not **13**
lift up so much as his eyes unto heaven, but
smote upon his breast, saying, God be merciful
to me a sinner.

I tell you, this man went down to his house jus- **14**
tified rather than the other; for every one that
exalteth himself shall be abased; and he that
humbleth himself shall be exalted.

Now it came to pass, as they went, that he **L. 10/38**
entered into a certain village: and a certain
woman, named Martha, received him into her
house.

And she had a sister called Mary, which also sat **39**
at Jesus' feet, and heard his word.

But Martha was cumbered about much serving, **40**
and came to him, and said, Lord, dost thou not

101

L. 10/40 care that my sister hath left me to serve alone? bid her therefore that she help me.

41 And Jesus answered and said unto her, Martha, Martha, thou art careful and troubled about many things:

42 But one thing is needful: and Mary hath chosen that good part, which shall not be taken away from her.

Mt. 19/1 And it came to pass, that when Jesus had finished these sayings, he departed from Galilee, and came into the coasts of Judaea beyond Jordan.

2 And great multitudes followed him;

3 The Pharisees also came unto him, tempting him, and saying unto him, Is it lawful for a man to put away his wife for every cause?

4 And he answered and said unto them, Have ye not read, that he which made them at the beginning made them male and female,

5 And said, For this cause shall a man leave father and mother, and shall cleave to his wife: and they twain shall be one flesh?

6 Wherefore they are no more twain, but one flesh. What therefore God hath joined together, let not man put asunder.

7 They say unto him, Why did Moses then command to give a writing of divorcement, and to put her away?

8 He saith unto them, Moses, because of the hard-

ness of your hearts suffered you to put away your **Mt. 19/8**
wives: but from the beginning it was not so.

And I say unto you, Whosoever shall put away **9**
his wife, except it be for fornication, and shall
marry another, committeth adultery: and whoso
marrieth her which is put away doth commit
adultery.

His disciples say unto him, If the case of the **10**
man be so with his wife, it is not good to marry.

1] But he said unto them, All men cannot receive **11**
this saying, save they to whom it is given.

For there are some eunuchs, which were so born **12**
from their*—of heaven's sake. He that is able to
receive it, let him receive it.

Then were there brought unto him little chil- **13**
dren, that he should put his hands on them, and
pray: and the disciples rebuked them.

But Jesus said, Suffer little children, and forbid **14**
them not, to come unto me: for of such is the
kingdom of heaven.

And he laid his hands on them, and departed **15**
thence.

And, behold, one came and said unto him, Good **16**

---

*Mr. Jefferson omitted from his English text the words:
"mother's womb; and there are some eunuchs, which were
made eunuchs of men; and there be eunuchs, which have
made themselves eunuchs for the kingdom…" Since the
passage is found in the parallel Greek, Latin and French
texts its omission here was doubtless due to inadvertence
which he did not take the trouble to correct.

Mt. 19/16 Master, what good thing shall I do, that I may have eternal life?

17 And he said unto him, Why callest thou me good? there is none good but one, that is God: but if thou wilt enter into life, keep the commandments.

18 He saith unto him, Which? Jesus said, Thou shalt do no murder, Thou shalt not commit adultery, Thou shalt not steal, Thou shalt not bear false witness,

19 Honour thy father and thy mother: and, Thou shalt love thy neighbour as thyself.

20 The young man saith unto him, All these things have I kept from my youth up: what lack I yet?

21 Jesus said unto him, If thou will be perfect, go and sell that thou hast and give to the poor, and thou shalt have treasure in heaven: and come and follow me.

22 But when the young man heard that saying, he went away sorrowful: for he had great possessions.

23 Then said Jesus unto his disciples, Verily I say unto you, That a rich man shall hardly enter into the kingdom of heaven.

24 And again I say unto you, It is easier for a camel to go through the eye of a needle, than for a rich man to enter into the kingdom of God.

25 When his disciples heard it, they were exceedingly amazed, saying, Who then can be saved?

But Jesus beheld them, and said unto them, **Mt. 19/26**
With men this is impossible; but with God all
things are possible.

For the kingdom of heaven is like unto a man **Mt. 20/1**
that is an householder, which went out early in
the morning to hire labourers into his vineyard.

And when he had agreed with the labourers for **2**
a penny a day, he sent them into his vineyard.

And he went out about the third hour, and saw **3**
others standing idle in the marketplace.

And said unto them; Go ye also into the vine- **4**
yard, and whatsoever is right I will give you.
And they went their way.

Again he went out about the sixth and ninth **5**
hour, and did likewise.

And about the eleventh hour he went out, and **6**
found others standing idle, and said unto them,
Why stand ye here all the day idle?

They say unto him, Because no man hath hired **7**
us. He saith unto them, Go ye also into the
vineyard; and whatsoever is right, that shall ye
receive.

So when even was come, the lord of the vine- **8**
yard saith unto his steward, Call the labourers,
and give them their hire, beginning from the
last unto the first.

And when they came that were hired about the **9**
eleventh hour, they received every man a
penny.

Mt. 20/10 But when the first came, they supposed that they should have received more; and they likewise received every man a penny.

11 And when they had received it, they murmured against the good man of the house,

12 Saying, these last have wrought but one hour, and thou hast made them equal unto us, which have borne the burden and heat of the day.

13 But he answered one of them and said, Friend, [5 I do thee no wrong: didst not thou agree with me for a penny?

14 Take that thine is, and go thy way: I will give unto this last even as unto thee.

15 Is it not lawful for me to do what I will with mine own? Is thine eye evil, because I am good?

16 So the last shall be first, and the first last: for many be called, but few chosen.

L. 19/1 And Jesus entered and passed through Jericho.

2 And, behold, there was a man named Zacchaeus, which was the chief among the publicans, and he was rich.

3 And he sought to see Jesus who he was; and could not for the press, because he was little of stature.

4 And he ran before, and climbed up into a sycamore tree to see him: for he was to pass that way.

5 And, when Jesus came to the place, he looked

up, and saw him, and said unto him, Zacchaeus, **L. 19/5**
make haste, and come down; for today I must
abide at thy house.

And he made haste, and came down, and re- **6**
ceived him joyfully.

And when they saw it, they all murmured, say- **7**
ing, That he was gone to be guest with a man
that is a sinner.

And Zacchaeus stood, and said unto the Lord; **8**
Behold, Lord, the half of my goods I give to
the poor; and if I have taken anything from
any man by false accusation, I restore him four-
fold.

And Jesus said unto him, This day is salvation **9**
come to this house, forsomuch as he also is a
son of Abraham.

For the Son of Man is come to seek and to save **10**
that which was lost.

And, as they heard these things, he added, and **11**
spake a parable, because he was nigh to Jerusalem, and because they thought that the kingdom of God should immediately appear.

He said therefore, A certain nobleman went into **12**
a far country to receive for himself a kingdom,
and to return.

And he called his ten servants, and delivered **13**
them ten pounds, and said unto them, Occupy
till I come.

But his citizens hated him, and sent a message **14**

L. 19/14 after him, saying, We will not have this man to reign over us.

15 And it came to pass, that when he was returned, having received the kingdom, then he commanded these servants to be called unto him, to whom he had given the money, that he might know how much every man had gained by trading.

16 Then came the first, saying, Lord, thy pound hath gained ten pounds.

17 And he said unto him, Well, thou good servant: because thou hast been faithful in a very little, have thou authority over ten cities.

18 And the second came, saying, Lord, thy pound hath gained five pounds.

19 And he said likewise to him, Be thou also over five cities.

20 And another came, saying, Lord, behold, here is thy pound, which I have kept laid up in a napkin:

21 For I feared thee, because thou art an austere man: thou takest up that thou layedst not down, and reapest that thou didst not sow.

22 And he saith unto him, Out of thine own mouth will I judge thee, thou wicked servant. Thou knewest that I was an austere man, taking up that I laid not down, and reaping that I did not sow:

23 Wherefore then gavest not thou my money into

the bank, that at my coming I might have re- **L. 19/23**
quired mine own with usury?

5] And he said unto them that stood by, take from **24**
him the pound, and give it to him that hath ten
pounds.

(And they said unto him, Lord, he hath ten **25**
pounds.)

For I say unto you, That unto every one which **26**
hath shall be given; and from him that hath
not, even that he hath shall be taken away from
him.

But those mine enemies, which would not that **27**
I should reign over them, bring hither, and slay
them before me.

And when he had thus spoken, he went before, **28**
ascending up to Jerusalem.

And when they drew nigh unto Jerusalem, **Mt. 21/1**
and were come to Bethphage, unto the
mount of Olives, then sent Jesus two
disciples,

Saying unto them, Go into the village over **2**
against you, and straightway ye shall find an ass
tied, and a colt with her: loose them, and bring
them unto me.

And if any man say aught unto you, ye shall **3**
say, The Lord hath need of them; and straightway he will send them.

And the disciples went, and did as Jesus com- **6**
manded them,

Mt. 21/7 And brought the ass, and the colt, and put on them their clothes, and they set him thereon.

8 And a very great multitude spread their garments in the way; others cut down branches from the trees, and strawed them in the way.

10 And when he was come into Jerusalem, all the city was moved, saying, Who is this?

J. 12/19 The Pharisees therefore said among themselves, Perceive ye how ye prevail nothing? behold, the world is gone after him.

20 And there were certain Greeks among them that came up to worship at the feast:

21 The same came therefore to Philip, which was of Bethsaida of Galilee, and desired him, saying, Sir, we would see Jesus.

22 Philip cometh and telleth Andrew: and again Andrew and Philip tell Jesus.

23 And Jesus answered them, saying,

24 Verily, verily, I say unto you, Except a corn of wheat fall into the ground and die, it abideth alone: but if it die, it bringeth forth much fruit.

Mt. 21/17 And he left them, and went out of the city into Bethany; and he lodged there.

Mk. 11/12 And on the morrow, when they were come from Bethany,

15 Jesus went into the temple, and began to cast out them that sold and bought in the temple, and overthrew the tables of the money-changers, and the seats of them that sold doves:

And would not suffer that any man should **Mk. 11/16**
carry any vessel through the temple.

And he taught, saying unto them, Is it not writ- **17**
ten, My house shall be called of all nations the
house of prayer? but ye have made it a den of
thieves.

And the scribes and chief priests heard it, and **18**
sought how they might destroy him: for they
feared him, because all the people was astonished at his doctrine.

And when even was come, he went out of the **19**
city.

[And they come again to Jerusalem: and he was **27**
walking in the temple, there come to him the
chief priests, and the scribes, and the elders,]*

And he said unto them, But what think ye? A **Mt. 21/28**
certain man had two sons; and he came to the
first, and said, Son, go work today in my vineyard.

He answered and said, I will not: but afterward **29**
he repented, and went.

And he came to the second, and said likewise. **30**
And he answered, and said, I go, sir: and went
not.

Whether of them twain did the will of his **31**
father? They say unto him, The first. Jesus saith

---

*The text does not give this verse but that Mr. Jefferson
intended to include it is indicated by his marginal note
reading "+ Mark 11.27."

Mt. 21/31 unto them, Verily I say unto you, That the publicans and the harlots go into the kingdom of God before you.

33 Hear another parable:

Mk. 12/1 A certain man planted a vineyard, and set an hedge about it, and digged a place for the winevat, and built a tower, and let it out to husbandmen, and went into a far country.

2 And at the season he sent to the husbandmen a servant, that he might receive from the husbandmen of the fruit of the vineyard.

3 And they caught him, and beat him, and sent him away empty.

4 And again he sent unto them another servant; and at him they cast stones, and wounded him in the head, and sent him away shamefully handled.

5 And again he sent another; and him they killed, and many others; beating some, and killing some.

6 Having yet therefore one son, his well-beloved, he sent him also last unto them, saying, They will reverence my son.

7 But those husbandmen said among themselves, This is the heir; come, let us kill him, and the inheritance shall be ours.

8 And they took him, and killed him, and cast him out of the vineyard.

[5

What shall therefore the lord of the vineyard **Mk. 12/9** do? he will come and destroy the husbandmen, and will give the vineyard unto others.

And when the chief priests and Pharisees had **Mt. 21/45** heard his parables, they perceived that he spake of them.

But when they sought to lay hands on him, they **46** feared the multitude, because they took him for a prophet.

And Jesus answered and spake unto them **Mt. 22/1** again by parables, and said,

The kingdom of heaven is like unto a **2** certain king, which made a marriage for his son.

And sent forth his servants to call them that **3** were bidden to the wedding: and they would not come.

Again, he sent forth other servants, saying, Tell **4** them which are bidden, Behold, I have prepared my dinner: my oxen and my fatlings are killed, and all things are ready: come unto the marriage.

But they made light of it, and went their ways, **5** one to his farm, another to his merchandise:

And the remnant took his servants and in- **6** treated them spitefully, and slew them.

But when the king heard thereof, he was wroth: **7** and he sent forth his armies, and destroyed those murderers, and burned up their city.

13

Mt. 22/8 Then saith he to his servants, The wedding is ready, but they which were bidden were not worthy.

9 Go ye therefore into the highways, and as many as ye shall find, bid to the marriage.

10 So those servants went out into the highways, and gathered together all as many as they found, both bad and good: and the wedding was furnished with guests.

11 And when the king came in to see the guests, he saw there a man which had not on a wedding garment:

12 And he saith unto him, Friend, how camest thou in hither not having a wedding garment? And he was speechless.

13 Then saith the king to the servants, Bind him hand and foot, and take him away, and cast him into outer darkness; there shall be weeping and gnashing of teeth.

14 For many are called, but few are chosen.

15 Then went the Pharisees, and took counsel how they might entangle him in his talk.

16 And they sent out unto him their disciples with the Herodians, saying, Master, we know that thou art true, and teachest the way of God in truth, neither carest thou for any man: for thou regardest not the person of men.

17 Tell us therefore, What thinkest thou? Is it lawful to give tribute unto Caesar, or not?

But Jesus perceived their wickedness, and said, **Mt. 22/18**
9] Why tempt ye me, ye hypocrites?

Shew me the tribute-money. And they brought **19**
unto him a penny.

And he saith unto them, Whose is this image **20**
and superscription?

They say unto him, Caesar's. Then saith he **21**
unto them, Render therefore unto Caesar the
things which are Caesar's; and unto God the
things that are God's.

When they had heard these words, they mar- **22**
velled, and left him, and went their way.

The same day came to him the Sadducees, which **23**
say that there is no resurrection, and asked him,

Saying, Master, Moses said, If a man die, having **24**
no children, his brother shall marry his wife,
and raise up seed unto his brother.

Now, there were with us seven brethren: and the **25**
first, when he had married a wife, deceased, and
having no issue, left his wife unto his brother:

Likewise the second also, and the third, unto **26**
the seventh.

And last of all the woman died also. **27**

Therefore, in the resurrection, whose wife shall
she be of the seven? for they all had her.

Jesus answered and said unto them, Ye do err, **29**
not knowing the scriptures, nor the power of
God.

For in the resurrection they neither marry, nor **30**

Mt. 22/30 are given in marriage; but are as the angels of God in heaven.

31 But as touching the resurrection of the dead, have ye not read that which was spoken unto you by God, saying,

32 I am the God of Abraham, and the God of Isaac, and the God of Jacob? God is not the God of the dead, but of the living.

33 And when the multitude heard this, they were astonished at his doctrine.

Mk. 12/28 And one of the scribes came, and having heard them reasoning together, and perceiving that he had answered them well, asked him, Which is the first commandment of all?

29 And Jesus answered him, The first of all the commandments is, Hear, O Israel; The Lord our God is one Lord:

30 And thou shalt love the Lord thy God with all thy heart, and with all thy soul, and with all thy mind, and with all thy strength. This is the first commandment.

31 And the second is like, namely this, Thou shalt love thy neighbour as thyself. There is none other commandment greater than these.

Mt. 22/40 On these two commandments hang all the law and the prophets.

Mk. 12/32 And the scribe said unto him, Well, Master thou hast said the truth: for there is one God and there is none other but he:

And to love him with all the heart, and with all **Mk. 12/33**
the understanding, and with all the soul, and
with all the strength, and to love his neighbour
as himself, is more than all whole burnt-offerings and sacrifices.

Then spake Jesus to the multitude, and to **Mt. 23/1**
his disciples,
Saying, The scribes and the Pharisees sit 2
in Moses' seat:

All therefore whatsoever they bid you observe, 3
that observe and do; but do not ye after their
works: for they say, and do not.

For they bind heavy burdens and grievous to be 4
borne, and lay them on men's shoulders; but
they themselves will not move them with one
of their fingers.

But all their works they do for to be seen of 5
men: they make broad their phylacteries, and
enlarge the borders of their garments.

And love the uppermost rooms at feasts, and 6
the chief seats in the synagogues,

And greetings in the markets, and to be called 7
of men, Rabbi, Rabbi.

But be not ye called Rabbi: for one is your 8
Master, even Christ; and all ye are brethren.

And call no man your father upon the earth: for 9
one is your Father, which is in heaven.

Neither be ye called masters: for one is your 10
Master, even Christ.

Mt. 23/11 But he that is greatest among you shall be your servant.

12 And whosoever shall exalt himself shall be abased; and he that shall humble himself shall be exalted.

13 But woe unto you, scribes and Pharisees, hypocrites! for ye shut up the kingdom of heaven against men: for ye neither go in yourselves, neither suffer ye them that are entering, to go in.

14 Woe unto you, scribes and Pharisees, hypocrites! for ye devour widows' houses, and for a pretence make long prayer: therefore ye shall receive the greater damnation.

15 Woe unto you, scribes and Pharisees, hypocrites! for ye compass sea and land to make one proselyte, and when he is made, ye make him twofold more the child of hell than yourselves.

16 Woe unto you, ye blind guides, which say, Whosoever shall swear by the temple, it is nothing; but whosoever shall swear by the gold of the temple, he is a debtor.

17 Ye fools and blind! for whether is greater, the gold, or the temple that sanctifieth the gold?

18 And, Whosoever shall swear by the altar, it is nothing; but whosoever sweareth by the gift that is upon it, he is guilty.

19 Ye fools and blind! for whether is greater, the gift, or the altar that sanctifieth the gift?

20 Whoso therefore shall swear by the altar, swear

eth by it, and by all things thereon.

Mt. 23/20

And whoso shall swear by the temple, sweareth 21
by it, and by him that dwelleth therein.

And he that shall swear by heaven, sweareth by 22
the throne of God, and by him that sitteth
thereon.

Woe unto you, scribes and Pharisees, hypo- 23
crites! for ye pay tithe of mint, and anise, and
cummin, and have omitted the weightier matters of the law, judgment, mercy, and faith:
these ought ye to have done, and not to leave
the other undone.

Ye blind guides! which strain at a gnat, and 24
swallow a camel.

Woe unto you, scribes and Pharisees, hypo- 25
crites! for ye make clean the outside of the cup
and of the platter, but within they are full of
extortion and excess.

Thou blind Pharisee, cleanse first that which is 26
within the cup and platter, that the outside of
them may be clean also.

Woe unto you, scribes and Pharisees, hypo- 27
crites! for ye are like unto whited sepulchres,
which indeed appear beautiful outward, but are
within full of dead men's bones, and of all un-
cleanness.

Even so ye also outwardly appear righteous 28
unto men, but within ye are full of hypocrisy
and iniquity.

Mt. 23/29 Woe unto you, scribes and Pharisees, hypocrites! because ye build the tombs of the prophets, and garnish the sepulchres of the righteous,

30 And say, If we had been in the days of our fathers, we would not have been partakers with them in the blood of the prophets.

31 Wherefore ye be witnesses unto yourselves, that ye are the children of them which killed the prophets.

32 Fill ye up then the measure of your fathers.

33 Ye serpents, ye generation of vipers! how can ye escape the damnation of hell?

Mk. 12/41 And Jesus sat over against the treasury, and beheld how the people cast money into the treasury: and many that were rich cast in much.

42 And there came a certain poor widow, and she threw in two mites, which make a farthing.

43 And he called unto him his disciples, and saith unto them, Verily I say unto you, That this poor widow hath cast more in, than all they which have cast into the treasury:

44 For all they did cast in of their abundance; but she of her want did cast in all that she had, even all her living.

Mt. 24/1 And Jesus went out, and departed from the temple: and his disciples came to him for to shew him the buildings of the temple. And Jesus said unto them, See ye not all these things? verily I say unto you, There shall not be

left here one stone upon another, that shall not **Mt. 24/2**
be thrown down.

Then let them which be in Judaea flee into the **16**
mountains:

Let him which is on the housetop not come **17**
down to take any thing out of his house:

Neither let him which is in the field return back **18**
to take his clothes.

And woe unto them that are with child, and to **19**
them that give suck in those days!

But pray ye that your flight be not in the win- **20**
ter, neither on the sabbath day:

For then shall be great tribulations, such as was **21**
not since the beginning of the world to this
time, no, nor ever shall be.

Immediately after the tribulation of those days **29**
shall the sun be darkened, and the moon shall
not give her light, and the stars shall fall from
heaven, and the powers of the heavens shall be
shaken.

Now learn a parable of the fig tree; When his **32**
branch is yet tender, and putteth forth leaves,
ye know that summer is nigh:

So likewise ye, when ye shall see all these **33**
things, know that it is near, even at the doors.

But of that day and hour knoweth no man, no, **36**
not the angels of heaven, but my Father only.

But as the days of Noe were so shall also the **37**
coming of the Son of Man be.

Mt. 24/38 For as in the days that were before the flood they were eating and drinking, marrying and giving in marriage, until the day that Noe entered into the ark,

39 And knew not until the flood came, and took them all away;

40 Then shall two be in the field; the one shall be taken, and the other left.

41 Two women shall be grinding at the mill; the one shall be taken and the other left.

42 Watch therefore: for ye know not what hour your Lord doth come.

43 But know this, that if the good man of the house had known in what watch the thief would come, he would have watched, and would not have suffered his house to be broken up.

44 Therefore be ye also ready:

45 Who then is a faithful and wise servant, whom his lord hath made ruler over his household, to give them meat in due season?

46 Blessed is that servant, whom his lord when he cometh shall find so doing.

47 Verily I say unto you, That he shall make him ruler over all his goods.

48 But and if that evil servant shall say in his heart, My lord delayeth his coming;

49 And shall begin to smite his fellowservants, and to eat and drink with the drunken;

50 The lord of that servant shall come in a day

122

when he looketh not for him, and in an hour **Mt. 24/50**
that he is not aware of,

And shall cut him asunder, and appoint him **51**
his portion with the hypocrites: there shall be
weeping and gnashing of teeth.

Then shall the kingdom of heaven be lik- **Mt. 25/1**
ened unto ten virgins, which took their
lamps, and went forth to meet the bridegroom.

And five of them were wise, and five were **2**
foolish.

They that were foolish took their lamps, and **3**
took no oil with them:

But the wise took oil in their vessels with their **4**
lamps.

While the bridegroom tarried, they all slum- **5**
bered and slept,

And at midnight there was a cry made, Behold, **6**
the bridegroom cometh; go ye out to meet him.

Then all those virgins arose, and trimmed their **7**
lamps.

And the foolish said unto the wise, Give us of **8**
your oil; for our lamps are gone out.

But the wise answered, saying, Not so; lest **9**
there be not enough for us and you: but go ye
rather to them that sell, and buy for yourselves.

And while they went to buy, the bridegroom **10**
came; and they that were ready went in with
him to the marriage: and the door was shut.

Mt. 25/11 Afterward came also the other virgins, saying, Lord, Lord, open to us.

12 But he answered and said, Verily I say unto you, I know you not.

13 Watch, therefore.

14 For the kingdom of heaven is as a man travelling into a far country, who called his own servants, and delivered unto them his goods.

15 And unto one he gave five talents, to another two, and to another one; to every man according to his several ability; and straightway took his journey. [6

16 Then he that had received the five talents went and traded with the same, and made them other five talents.

17 And likewise he that had received two, he also gained other two.

18 But he that had received one went and digged in the earth, and hid his lord's money.

19 After a long time the lord of those servants cometh, and reckoneth with them.

20 And so he that had received five talents came and brought other five talents, saying, Lord, thou deliveredst unto me five talents: behold, I have gained beside them five talents more.

21 His lord said unto him, Well done, thou good and faithful servant: thou hast been faithful over a few things, I will make thee ruler over many things: enter thou into the joy of thy lord.

He also that had received two talents came and **Mt. 25/22**
said, Lord, thou deliveredst unto me two talents: behold, I have gained two other talents
beside them.

His lord said unto him, Well done, good and **23**
faithful servant; thou hast been faithful over a
few things, I will make thee ruler over many
things: enter thou into the joy of thy lord.

Then he which had received the one talent came **24**
and said, Lord, I knew thee that thou art
an hard man, reaping where thou hast not
sown, and gathering where thou hast not
strawed:

And I was afraid, and went and hid thy talent **25**
in the earth: lo, there thou hast that is thine.

His lord answered and said unto him, Thou **26**
wicked and slothful servant, thou knewest that
I reap where I sowed not, and gather where I
have not strawed:

Thou oughtest therefore to have put my money **27**
to the exchangers, and then at my coming I
should have received mine own with usury.

Take therefore the talent from him, and give it **28**
unto him which hath ten talents.

For unto every one that hath shall be given, **29**
and he shall have abundance: but from him
that hath not shall be taken away even that
which he hath.

And cast ye the unprofitable servant into outer **30**

Mt. 25/30   darkness: there shall be weeping and gnashing of teeth.

L. 21/34   And take heed to yourselves, lest at any time your hearts be overcharged with surfeiting, and drunkenness, and cares of this life, and so that day come upon you unawares.

35   For as a snare shall it come on all them that dwell on the face of the whole earth.

36   Watch ye therefore, and pray always, that ye may be accounted worthy to escape all these things that shall come to pass, and to stand before the Son of Man.

Mt. 25/31   When the Son of Man shall come in his glory, and all the holy angels with him, then shall he sit upon the throne of his glory:

32   And before him shall be gathered all nations: and he shall separate them one from another, as a shepherd divideth his sheep from the goats:

33   And he shall set the sheep on his right hand, but the goats on the left.

34   Then shall the King say unto them on his right hand, Come, ye blessed of my Father, inherit the kingdom prepared for you from the foundation of the world:

35   For I was an hungered, and ye gave me meat: I was thirsty, and ye gave me drink: I was a stranger, and ye took me in:

36   Naked, and ye clothed me: I was sick, and ye visited me: I was in prison, and ye came unto me.

126

58] Then shall the righteous answer him, saying, **Mt. 25/37**
Lord, when saw we thee an hungered, and fed
thee? or thirsty, and gave thee drink?

When saw we thee a stranger, and took thee in? **38**
or naked, and clothed thee?

Or when saw we thee sick, or in prison, and **39**
came unto thee?

And the King shall answer and say unto them, **40**
Verily I say unto you, Inasmuch as ye have
done it unto one of the least of these my
brethren, ye have done it unto me.

Then shall he say also unto them on the left **41**
hand, Depart from me, ye cursed, into everlasting fire, prepared for the devil and his angels:

For I was an hungered, and ye gave me no meat: **42**
I was thirsty, and ye gave me no drink:

I was a stranger, and ye took me not in: naked, **43**
and ye clothed me not: sick, and in prison, and
ye visited me not.

Then shall they also answer him, saying, Lord, **44**
when saw we thee an hungered, or athirst, or a
stranger, or naked, or sick, or in prison, and did
not minister unto thee?

Then shall he answer them, saying, Verily I say **45**
unto you, Inasmuch as ye did it not to one of
the least, ye did it not to me.

And these shall go away into everlasting pun- **46**
ishment: but the righteous into life eternal.

After two days was the feast of the passover, **Mk. 14/1**

Mk. 14/1 and of unleavened bread: and the chief priests and the scribes sought how they might take him by craft, and put him to death.

2 But they said, Not on the feast day, lest there be an uproar of the people.

3 And being in Bethany in the house of Simon the leper, as he sat at meat, there came a woman, having an alabaster box of ointment of spike- [6 nard very precious; and she brake the box, and poured it on his head.

4 And there were some that had indignation within themselves, and said, Why was this waste of the ointment made?

5 For it might have been sold for more than three hundred pence, and have been given to the poor. And they murmured against her.

6 And Jesus said, Let her alone; why trouble ye her? she hath wrought a good work on me.

7 For ye have the poor with you always, and whensoever ye will ye may do them good: but me ye have not always.

8 She hath done what she could: she is come aforehand to anoint my body to the burying.

Mt. 26/14 Then one of the twelve, called Judas Iscariot, went unto the chief priests,

15 And said unto them, What will ye give me, and I will deliver him unto you? And they covenanted with him for thirty pieces of silver.

128

And from that time he sought opportunity to betray him. Mt. 26/16

Now the first day of the feast of unleavened bread the disciples came to Jesus, saying unto him, Where wilt thou that we prepare for thee to eat the passover? 17

And he said, Go into the city to such a man, and say unto him, The Master saith, My time is at hand; I will keep the passover at thy house with my disciples. 18

And the disciples did as Jesus had appointed them; and they made ready the passover. 19

Now when the even was come, he sat down with the twelve. 20

And there was also a strife among them, which of them should be accounted the greatest, L. 22/24

And he said unto them, The kings of the Gentiles exercise lordship over them; and they that exercise authority upon them are called benefactors. 25

But ye shall not be so: but he that is greatest among you, let him be as the younger: and he that is chief, as he that doth serve. 26

For whether is greater, he that sitteth at meat, or he that serveth? is not he that sitteth at meat? but I am among you as he that serveth. 27

And supper being ended, J. 13/2

He riseth from supper, and laid aside his gar- 4

J. 13/4 ments; and took a towel, and girded himself.

5 After that he poureth water into a basin, and began to wash the disciples' feet, and to wipe them with the towel wherewith he was girded.

6 Then cometh he to Simon Peter: and Peter saith unto him, Lord, dost thou wash my feet?

7 Jesus answered and said unto him, What I do thou knowest not now; but thou shalt know hereafter.

8 Peter saith unto him, Thou shalt never wash my feet. Jesus answered him, If I wash thee not, thou hast no part with me.

9 Simon Peter saith unto him, Lord, not my feet only, but also my hands and my head.

10 Jesus saith to him, He that is washed needeth not save to wash his feet, but is clean every whit: and ye are clean, but not all.

11 For he knew who should betray him; therefore said he, Ye are not all clean.

12 So after he had washed their feet, and had taken his garments, and was set down again, he said unto them, Know ye what I have done to you?

13 Ye call me Master and Lord: and ye say well; for so I am.

14 If I then, your Lord and Master, have washed your feet; ye also ought to wash one another's feet.

15 For I have given you an example, that ye should do as I have done to you.

Verily, verily, I say unto you, The servant is **J. 13/16** not greater than his lord; neither he that is sent, greater than he that sent him.

If ye know these things, happy are ye if ye do **17** them.

1] When Jesus had thus said, he was troubled in **21** spirit, and testified, and said, Verily, verily, I say unto you, that one of you shall betray me.

Then the disciples looked one on another, **22** doubting of whom he spake.

Now there was leaning on Jesus' bosom one of **23** his disciples, whom Jesus loved.

Simon Peter therefore beckoned to him, that he **24** should ask who it should be of whom he spake.

He then lying on Jesus' breast saith unto him, **25** Lord, who is it?

Jesus answered, He it is, to whom I shall give a **26** sop, when I have dipped it. And when he had dipped the sop, he gave it to Judas Iscariot, the son of Simon.

Therefore, when he was gone out, Jesus said: **31**

A new commandment I give unto you, That ye **34** love one another; as I have loved you, that ye also love one another.

By this shall all men know that ye are my dis- **35** ciples, if ye have love one to another.

Then saith Jesus unto them, All ye shall be of- **Mt. 26/31** fended because of me this night:

Peter answered and said unto him, Though all **33**

131

Mt. 26/33 men shall be offended because of thee, yet will I never be offended.

L. 22/33 I am ready to go with thee, both into prison, and to death.

34 And he said, I tell thee, Peter, the cock shall not crow this day before that thou shalt thrice deny that thou knowest me.

Mt. 26/35 Peter said unto him, Though I should die with thee, yet will I not deny thee. Likewise also said all the disciples.

36 Then cometh Jesus with them unto a place called Gethsemane, and saith unto the disciples, Sit ye here, while I go and pray yonder.

37 And he took with him Peter and the two sons of Zebedee, and began to be sorrowful and very heavy.

38 Then saith he unto them, My soul is exceeding sorrowful, even unto death: tarry ye here, and watch with me.

39 And he went a little farther, and fell on his face, and prayed, saying, O my Father, if it be possible, let this cup pass from me: nevertheless not as I will, but as thou wilt.

40 And he cometh unto the disciples, and findeth them asleep, and saith unto Peter, What! could ye not watch with me one hour?

41 Watch and pray, that ye enter not into temptation: the spirit indeed is willing, but the flesh is weak.

He went away again the second time, and **Mt. 26/42** prayed, saying, O my Father, if this cup may not pass away from me, except I drink it, thy will be done.

And he came and found them asleep again: for **43** their eyes were heavy.

And he left them, and went away again, and **44** prayed the third time, saying the same words.

Then cometh he to his disciples, and saith unto **45** them, Sleep on now, and take your rest.

When Jesus had spoken these words, he **J. 18/1** went forth with his disciples over the brook Cedron, where was a garden, into the which he entered, and his disciples.

And Judas also, which betrayed him, knew the **2** place: for Jesus ofttimes resorted thither with his disciples.

Judas then, having received a band of men and **3** officers from the chief priests and Pharisees, cometh thither with lanterns, and torches and weapons.

Now that he betrayed him gave them a sign, **Mt. 26/48** saying, Whomsoever I shall kiss, that same is he: hold him fast.

And forthwith he came to Jesus, and said, Hail, **49** Master, and kissed him.

And Jesus said unto him, Friend, wherefore art **50** thou come?

Jesus therefore, knowing all things that should **J. 18/4**

J. 18/4 come upon him, went forth, and said unto them, Whom seek ye?

5 They answered him, Jesus of Nazareth. Jesus saith unto them, I am he. (And Judas also, which betrayed him, stood with them.)

6 As soon then as he had said unto them, I am he, they went backward, and fell to the ground.

7 Then asked he them again, Whom seek ye? And they said, Jesus of Nazareth.

8 Jesus answered, I have told you that I am he: if, therefore, ye seek me, let these go their way:

Mt. 26/50 Then came they, and laid hands on Jesus and took him.

51 And, behold, one of them which were with Jesus stretched out his hand, and drew his sword, and struck a servant of the high priest, and smote off his ear.

52 Then said Jesus unto him, Put up again thy sword into his place: for all they that take the sword shall perish with the sword.

55 In that same hour said Jesus to the multitudes, Are ye come out as against a thief with swords and staves for to take me? I sat daily with you teaching in the temple, and ye laid no hold on me.

56 Then all the disciples forsook him, and fled.

Mk. 14/51 And there followed him a certain young man, having a linen cloth cast about his naked body: and the young men laid hold on him:

134

And he left the linen cloth, and fled from them naked. **Mk. 14/52**

4] And they that had laid hold on Jesus led him away to Caiaphas the high priest, where the scribes and the elders were assembled. **Mt. 26/57**

And Simon Peter followed Jesus, and so did another disciple: that disciple was known unto the high priest, and went in with Jesus into the palace of the high priest. **J. 18/15**

But Peter stood at the door without. Then went out that other disciple, which was known unto the high priest, and spake unto her that kept the door, and brought in Peter. **16**

And the servants and officers stood there, who had made a fire of coals; for it was cold: and they warmed themselves: and Peter stood with them, and warmed himself. **18**

Then saith the damsel that kept the door unto Peter, Art not thou also one of this man's disciples? He saith, I am not. **17**

And Simon Peter stood and warmed himself: they said, therefore, unto him, Art not thou also one of his disciples? He denied it, and said, I am not. **25**

One of the servants of the high priest, (being his kinsman whose ear Peter cut off,) saith, Did not I see thee in the garden with him? **26**

Peter then denied again: and immediately the cock crew. **27**

Mt. 26/75 And Peter remembered the words of Jesus, which said unto him, Before the cock crow, thou shalt deny me thrice. And he went out, and wept bitterly.

J. 18/19 The high priest then asked Jesus of his disciples, and of his doctrine.

20 Jesus answered him, I spake openly to the world; I ever taught in the synagogue, and in the temple, whither the Jews always resort; and in secret have I said nothing.

21 Why askest thou me? ask them which heard [' me, what I have said unto them: behold, they know what I said.

22 And when he had thus spoken, one of the officers which stood by struck Jesus with the palm of his hand, saying, Answerest thou the high priest so?

23 Jesus answered him, If I have spoken evil, bear witness of the evil: but if well, why smitest thou me?

Mk. 14/53 And they led Jesus away to the high priest: and with him were assembled all the chief priests and the elders and the scribes.*

55 And the chief priests and all the council sought for witness against Jesus to put him to death; and found none:

---

*Mr. Jefferson included this verse in the English text but omitted it from the Greek, Latin and French texts, and from the Table of Contents.

For many bare false witness against him, but their witness agreed not together.   Mk. 14/56

And there arose certain, and bare false witness against him, saying,   57

We heard him say, I will destroy this temple that is made with hands, and within three days I will build another made without hands.   58

But neither so did their witness agree together.   59

And the high priest stood up in the midst, and   60

asked Jesus, saying, Answerest thou nothing?   61
what is it which these witness against thee?

But he held his peace, and answered nothing. Again the high priest asked him, and said unto him, Art thou the Christ, the Son of the Blessed?

And he said unto them, If I tell you, ye will not believe: L. 22/67

And if I also ask you, ye will not answer me, nor let me go.   68

Then said they all, Art thou then the Son of God? And he said unto them, Ye say that I am.   70

Then the high priest rent his clothes, and saith, What need we any further witnesses?   Mk. 14/63

Ye have heard the blasphemy: what think ye?   64
And they all condemned him to be guilty of death.

And some began to spit on him, and to cover his face, and to buffet him, and to say unto him, Prophesy: and the servants did strike him with the palms of their hands.   65

J. 18/28 Then they led Jesus from Caiaphas unto the hall of judgment, and it was early; and they themselves went not into the judgment hall, lest they should be defiled; but that they might eat the passover.

29 Pilate then went out unto them, and said, What accusation bring ye against this man?

30 They answered and said unto him, If he were not a malefactor, we would not have delivered him up unto thee.

31 Then said Pilate unto them, Take ye him, and judge him according to your law. The Jews therefore said unto him, It is not lawful for us to put any man to death:

33 Then Pilate entered into the judgment hall again, and called Jesus, and said unto him, Art thou the King of the Jews?

34 Jesus answered him, Sayest thou this thing of thyself, or did others tell it thee of me?

35 Pilate answered, Am I a Jew? Thine own nation and the chief priests have delivered thee unto me: what hast thou done?

36 Jesus answered, My kingdom is not of this world. If my kingdom were of this world, then would my servants fight, that I should not be delivered to the Jews: but now is my kingdom not from hence.

37 Pilate therefore said unto him, Art thou a king then? Jesus answered, Thou sayest that I am a

king. To this end was I born, and for this cause **J. 18/37**
came I into the world, that I should bear witness unto the truth. Everyone that is of the
truth heareth my voice.

Pilate saith unto him, What is truth? And when **38**
he had said this, he went out again unto the
Jews, and saith unto them, I find in him no fault
at all.

] And they were more fierce, saying, He stirreth **L. 23/5**
up the people, teaching throughout all Jewry,
beginning from Galilee to this place.

Then said Pilate unto him, Hearest thou not **Mt. 27/13**
how many things they witness against thee?

When Pilate heard of Galilee, he asked whether **L. 23/6**
the man were a Galilaean.

And as soon as he knew that he belonged unto **7**
Herod's jurisdiction, he sent him to Herod, who
himself also was at Jerusalem at that time.

And when Herod saw Jesus, he was exceeding **8**
glad: for he was desirous to see him of a long
season, because he had heard many things of
him; and he hoped to have seen some miracle
done by him.

Then he questioned with him in many words; **9**
but he answered him nothing.

And the chief priests and scribes stood and **10**
vehemently accused him.

And Herod, with his men of war, set him at **11**
nought and mocked him, and arrayed him in a

L. 23/11 gorgeous robe, and sent him again to Pilate.

12 And the same day Pilate and Herod were made friends together: for before they were at enmity between themselves.

13 And Pilate, when he had called together the chief priests and the rulers and the people,

14 Said unto them, Ye have brought this man unto me, as one that perverteth the people:* and, behold, I, having examined him before you, have found no fault in this man touching those things whereof ye accuse him:

15 No, nor yet Herod: for I sent you to him; and, lo, nothing worthy of death is done unto him.

16 I will, therefore, chastise him, and release him.

Mt. 27/15 Now at that feast the governor was wont to release unto the people a prisoner, whom they would.

16 And they had then a notable prisoner, called Barabbas.

17 Therefore when they were gathered together, Pilate said unto them, Whom will ye that I release unto you? Barabbas, or Jesus which is called Christ?

---

*[A footnote in Mr. Jefferson's handwriting so small as to be almost illegible, and with some words doubtful, reads,] under the Roman law de seditiosis in crucem tollendis. "Digest de poenis L. 48, lit. 19.6. 28.3." capita plectandi cum saepius seditiosa et turbulentia se gesserint, et aliquotione adprehensi clementius in eadem tementate propositi persevenaverint?

For he knew that for envy they had delivered him. **Mt. 27/18**

When he was set down on the judgment seat, **19** his wife sent unto him, saying, Have thou nothing to do with that just man: for I have suffered many things this day in a dream because of him.

But the chief priests and elders persuaded the **20** multitude that they should ask Barabbas, and destroy Jesus.

The governor answered and said unto them, **21** Whether of the twain will ye that I release unto you? They said, Barabbas.

Pilate saith unto them, What shall I do then **22** with Jesus which is called Christ? They all say unto him, Let him be crucified.

And the governor said, Why, what evil hath he **23** done? But they cried out the more, saying, Let him be crucified.

Then released he Barabbas unto them: and when **26** he had scourged Jesus, he delivered him to be crucified.

Then the soldiers of the governor took Jesus **27** into the common hall, and gathered unto him the whole band of soldiers.

And when they had platted a crown of thorns, **29** they put it upon his head, and a reed in his right hand: and they bowed the knee before him, and mocked him, saying, Hail, King of the Jews!

Mt. 27/30 And they spit upon him, and took the reed, and smote him on the head.

31 And after that they had mocked him, they took the robe off from him, and put his own raiment on him, and led him away to crucify him.

3 Then Judas, which had betrayed him, when he [saw that he was condemned, repented himself, and brought again the thirty pieces of silver to the chief priests and elders,

4 Saying, I have sinned in that I have betrayed the innocent blood. And they said, What is that to us? see thou to that.

5 And he cast down the pieces of silver in the temple and departed, and went and hanged himself.

6 And the chief priests took the silver pieces, and said, It is not lawful for to put them into the treasury, because it is the price of blood.

7 And they took counsel, and bought with them the potter's field, to bury strangers in.

8 Wherefore that field was called, The field of blood, unto this day.

L. 23/26 And as they led him away, they laid hold upon one Simon, a Cyrenian, coming out of the country, and on him they laid the cross, that he might bear it after Jesus.

27 And there followed him a great company of people, and of women, which also bewailed and lamented him.

28 But Jesus turning unto them said, Daughters of

Jerusalem, weep not for me, but weep for your-   **L. 23/28**
selves, and for your children.

For, behold, the days are coming, in the which   **29**
they shall say, Blessed are the barren, and the
wombs that never bare, and the paps which
never gave suck.

Then shall they begin to say to the mountains,   **30**
Fall on us; and to the hills, Cover us.

For if they do these things in a green tree, what   **31**
shall be done in the dry?

And there were also two others, malefactors,   **32**
led with him to be put to death.

And he bearing his cross went forth into a place   **J. 19/17**
called the place of a skull, which is called in
the Hebrew, Golgotha:

Where they crucified him, and two other with   **18**
him, on either side one, and Jesus in the midst.

And Pilate wrote a title, and put it on the cross.   **19**
And the writing was, JESUS OF NAZARETH,
THE KING OF THE JEWS.

This title then read many of the Jews: for the   **20**
place where Jesus was crucified was nigh to the
city: and it was written in Hebrew, and Greek,
and Latin.

Then said the chief priests of the Jews to Pilate,   **21**
Write not, The King of the Jews; but that he
said, I am King of the Jews.

Pilate answered, What I have written I have   **22**
written.

J. 19/23 Then the soldiers, when they had crucified Jesus, took his garments, and made four parts, to every soldier a part; and also his coat: now the coat was without seam, woven from the top throughout.

24 They said therefore among themselves, Let us not rend it, but cast lots for it, whose it shall be:

Mt. 27/39 And they that passed by reviled him, wagging their heads,

40 And saying, Thou that destroyest the temple and buildest it in three days, save thyself. If thou be the Son of God, come down from the cross.

41 Likewise also the chief priests mocking him, with the scribes and elders said,

42 He saved others; himself he cannot save. If he be the King of Israel, let him now come down from the cross, and we will believe him.

43 He trusted in God; let him deliver him now, if he will have him: for he said, I am the Son of God.

L. 23/39 And one of the malefactors which were hanged railed on him, saying, If thou be Christ, save thyself and us.

40 But the other answering rebuked him, saying, Dost not thou fear God, seeing thou art in the same condemnation?

41 And we indeed justly; for we receive the due

14

reward of our deeds: but this man hath done **L. 23/41**
nothing amiss.

Then said Jesus, Father, forgive them; for they **34**
know not what they do.

Now there stood by the cross of Jesus his **J. 19/25**
mother, and his mother's sister, Mary the wife
of Cleophas, and Mary Magdalene.

When Jesus therefore saw his mother, and the **26**
disciple standing by, whom he loved, he saith
unto his mother, Woman, behold thy Son!

Then saith he to the disciple, Behold thy **27**
mother! And from that hour that disciple took
her unto his own home.

And about the ninth hour Jesus cried with a **Mt. 27/46**
loud voice, saying, Eli, Eli, lama sabachthani?
that is to say, My God, My God, why hast thou
forsaken me?

Some of them that stood there, when they **47**
heard that, said, This man calleth for Elias.

And straightway one of them ran, and took a **48**
spunge, and filled it with vinegar and put it on
a reed, and gave him to drink.

The rest said, Let be, let us see whether Elias **49**
will come to save him.

Jesus, when he had cried again with a loud **50**
voice, yielded up the ghost.

And many women were there beholding afar **55**
off, which followed Jesus from Galilee, min-
istering unto him.

Mt. 27/56 Among which was Mary Magdalene, and Mary the mother of James and Joses, and the mother of Zebedee's children.

J. 19/31 The Jews, therefore, because it was the prepara- [s tion, that the bodies should not remain upon the cross on the sabbath day, (for that sabbath day was an high day,) besought Pilate that their legs might be broken, and that they might be taken away.

32 Then came the soldiers, and brake the legs of and first, and of the other which was crucified with him.

33 But when they came to Jesus, and saw that he was dead already, they brake not his legs:

34 But one of the soldiers with a spear pierced his side, and forthwith came thereout blood and water.

38 And after this Joseph of Arimathaea, (being a disciple of Jesus, but secretly for fear of the Jews,) besought Pilate that he might take away the body of Jesus: and Pilate gave him leave. He came therefore, and took the body of Jesus.

39 And there came also Nicodemus, (which at the first came to Jesus by night,) and brought a mixture of myrrh and aloes, about an hundred pound weight.

40 Then took they the body of Jesus, and wound it in linen clothes with the spices, as the manner of the Jews is to bury.

Now, in the place where he was crucified, there J. 19/41
was a garden; and in the garden a new sepulchre,
wherein was never man yet laid.

There laid they Jesus, 42

And rolled a great stone to the door of the Mt. 27/60
sepulchre, and departed.

Jefferson

AND HIS CONTEMPORARIES

JAROSLAV PELIKAN

There has certainly never been a shortage of boldness in the history of biblical scholarship during the past two centuries, but for sheer audacity Thomas Jefferson's two redactions of the Gospels stand out even in that company. It is still a bit overwhelming to contemplate the sangfroid exhibited by the third president of the United States as, razor in hand, he sat editing the Gospels during February 1804, on (as he himself says) "2. or 3. nights only at Washington, after getting thro' the evening task of reading the letters and papers of the day." He was apparently quite sure that he could tell what was genuine and what was not in the transmitted text of the New Testament, and the eventual outcome of his research and reflection is presented here in this volume. As Dickinson Adams put it after studying Jefferson's procedures, "although many distinguished biblical scholars have been daunted by the challenge of disentangling the many layers of the New Testament, the rationalistic Jefferson was supremely confident of his ability to differentiate between the true and the false precepts of Jesus."

In Jefferson's two excursions into New Testament study, *The Philosophy of Jesus of Nazareth* and then, almost two decades later, this version of *The Life and Morals of Jesus of Nazareth Extracted textually from the Gospels in Greek, Latin, French & English*, historical and literary judgments interact with religious and theological ones. The form in which our Gospels were composed by their anonymous authors (the names Matthew, Mark, Luke, and John appearing only in superscriptions which were presumably added later) makes the task of reconciling their narratives both unavoidable and difficult. Already in the second century, Tatian had prepared a combination of the four accounts, usually called *Diatessaron* ("[one] out of four"), which would enjoy quasi-canonical standing in the Syriac church for centuries; and around the year 400 Augustine prepared *De consensu evangelistarum*, often called his "most laborious work," to prove that the Gospel histories did not contradict one another.

Yet unless one is prepared, as Andreas Osiander apparently was in his *Four Books of the Harmony of the Gospels* (Basel, 1537), to regard even the slightest difference between these four accounts as evidence of separate incidents, one is compelled to assume that not all four Gospels, or perhaps even not a single one of the Gospels, can be strictly chronological in their narration. How long did the public ministry of Jesus last, the year or so suggested by the first three Gospels or the three years or so indicated by the sequence of Jewish festivals in the Fourth Gospel? Did he drive the money changers out of the Temple of Jerusalem at the beginning of his career as a teacher (John 2:13–17) or in its final week (Matt. 21:12–13; Mark 11:15–17; Luke 19:45–46), or did he perhaps do it twice? Is the Sermon on the Mount (Matt. 5–7) identical with the Sermon on the Plain (Luke 6:20–49)? And just how many "words on the Cross" were there, the seven that have been hallowed by various musical settings and homiletical-devotional expositions or the less determinate number that comes from a comparison of the Gospel stories, including the intriguing textual variants?

Regardless of dogmatic presuppositions, or for that matter of antidogmatic presuppositions, therefore, every serious reader of the New Testament is confronted with a host of problems in trying to make historical sense of "the life and morals of Jesus of Nazareth." How such a reader copes with those problems will depend on the interaction of various factors,

151

some of them historiographical and some of them theological (and most of them both historiographical and theological). That neither theological orthodoxy nor a reverence for the inspired text has precluded "tampering" can be seen in the variants of the story of the boy Jesus in the Temple, which appears in the second chapter of the Gospel according to Luke. The Greek text quite unambiguously has Mary say to Jesus: "Behold, your father and I have been looking for you anxiously." But that did not prevent a few pious scribes from deciding, in the light of the story of the Annunciation contained in the preceding chapter, that "your father and I" should be replaced by "we," to avoid any impression that Joseph was in fact the natural father of Jesus.

Even a literalistic adherence to "the original text," moreover, does not dispose of the problems, though it does manage to raise a host of new ones. Thus the *pericope adulteriae*, the story of the woman caught in the act of adultery and dragged before Jesus for his judgment, is evidently not an authentic part of that "original text." Printing the story at the beginning of the eighth chapter of the Gospel of John, the Revised Standard Version explains in a footnote: "The most ancient authorities omit 7.53–8.11; other authorities add the passage here or after

7.36 or after 21.25 or after Luke 21.38, with variations of text." Nevertheless, many scholars are convinced that the incident validates itself *prima facie* as an authentic element of the earliest tradition about Jesus, and that it was not, despite the textual problems, a later addition by a church in which, increasingly, many followers of Jesus were showing that they would have been quite willing to "cast the first stone."

Although he did have a keen interest in all sorts of antiquarian questions, Jefferson was not engaging in a "quest for the historical Jesus" primarily as an exercise in historical investigation, any more than were most of the others who participated in that quest during the nineteenth and twentieth centuries. He wanted to find the essence of true religion in the Gospels, an essence whose basic content he had already formulated for himself with considerable simplicity and clarity. Like other Enlightenment rationalists, Jefferson was convinced that the real villain in the Christian story was the apostle Paul, who had corrupted the religion *of* Jesus into a religion *about* Jesus, which thus had, in combination with the otherworldly outlook of the Fourth Gospel, produced the monstrosities of dogma, superstition, and priestcraft, which were the essence of Christian orthodoxy. The essence of authentic religion, and therefore of the only kind of Christianity in which Jefferson was interested, needed to be rescued from these distortions, so that the true person and teaching of Jesus of Nazareth might rise from the dead page—the only kind of resurrection Jefferson was prepared to accept.

It has become customary in our time to speak rather condescendingly about this search for an "essence" within and behind the received forms of the Christian message, with such pejorative terms as "reductionism" springing easily to mind. Yet it bears pointing out that the search is in fact an ancient one, and that it comes with some very impressive credentials. "He has showed you, O man, what is good; and what does the Lord require of you but to do justice, and to love kindness, and to walk humbly with your God?" the prophet Micah declared. The writer of the Epistle to the Hebrews likewise asserted that "whoever would draw near to God must believe that he exists and that he rewards those who seek him." And when Jesus was approached with the stock rabbinical question about which was the great commandment in the law, he did not, according to the Gospels, reject the question as reductionist, but stood it on its head by making love to God and love to neighbor coordinate. This is not to say that Jefferson's version of the "essence" is automatically legitimate, but the impulse to look for an irreducible minimum in the welter of belief and practice cannot be waved aside as reductionism.

The Enlightenment of the eighteenth century, of which Thomas Jefferson was in his own highly individual fashion both a pupil and an exponent, brought to this assignment a new interest in history as an instrument for clarification and liberation. In the well-known contrast drawn by his contemporary, Edward Gibbon, "the theologian may indulge the pleasing task of describing Religion as she descended from Heaven, arrayed in her native purity. A more melancholy duty is imposed on the historian. He must discover the inevitable mixture of error and corruption which she contracted in a long residence upon earth, among a weak and degenerate race of beings"; Gibbon left no doubt about where his own sympathies lay between the two, and they were sympathies that Jefferson shared. And when, moreover, Gibbon described history as "indeed, little more than the register of the crimes, follies, and misfortunes of mankind," that, too, at least as it pertained to most ancient monarchies and institutional churches, was a sentiment in which Jefferson would have concurred. It was the historian's task to penetrate the layers of myth and propaganda and to find the real truth of history.

Applied to the history of Christianity, that task entailed the abolition of the privileged sanctuary in which the writers and events of the Bible had been reposing for centuries, as well as the application to them of the same critical methodologies that pertained to any honest historiography. Significantly, that principle was easier and "safer" to carry out in studying the Old Testament than the New, and within the New Testament in interpreting the Epistles than in analyzing the Gospels. Not without touches of anti-Semitic condescension, radical critics set the "tribal religion of Jehovah" into opposition with the higher and more universal (that is to say, more rationalistic and less specifically Jewish) religion allegedly espoused by the Minor Prophets. They went on to draw a similar opposition between the universal religion of Jesus and the Christian particularity of the religion of Paul. Combining these two emphases, Jefferson thus made Jesus into "the greatest of all the Reformers of the depraved religion of his own country," but Paul into the "first corrupter of the doctrines of Jesus."

To put this version of *The Life and Morals of Jesus of Nazareth* into historical context, it is in-

structive to compare the approach of Thomas
Jefferson (1734–1826) to the central issues
with those of several of his contemporaries,
older and younger, who likewise addressed
themselves to these issues. In chronological order, they are Hermann Samuel Reimarus
(1694–1768), David Hume (1711–76), Johann
Wolfgang von Goethe (1749–1832), and John
Henry Newman (1801–90).

Of the four, Hermann Samuel Reimarus was
the closest to Jefferson in the intellectual and
scholarly enterprise of probing for the real man
Jesus of Nazareth behind the figure in the Gospels. It is noteworthy that Albert Schweitzer's
The Quest of the Historical Jesus begins with him;
the German title of Schweitzer's book is *Von
Reimarus zu Wrede.* Reimarus did not, however,
carry out his own reconstruction of "the life
and morals of Jesus of Nazareth" by resorting
to the draconian measure of expunging from
the text what apparently did not belong there,
so as, in Jefferson's choice phrase, to separate
the "diamonds" from the "dung." Instead, Reimarus labored for many years on an *Apology or
Defense of the Rational Worshipers of God* (a title
that Jefferson would have found congenial), the
fundamental section of which bore the title:
"On the Intention of Jesus and of His Disciples." As Reimarus read the story, the teach-

157

ings of Jesus were an uneasy amalgam of a universal, rational religion with remnants of the religion of Israel. His "intention," accordingly, also combined a message of the pure, nonceremonial worship of the one God with a belief in apocalyptic intervention by the God of Israel and a consequent establishment of the kingdom of God on earth. This kingdom, Jesus believed, would come into being through him. To that belief he clung to the very end, and the cry of dereliction on the cross, "My God, my God, why hast thou forsaken me?" with its echoes of Psalm 22, was his heartbroken scream of despair when he finally had to recognize that the theocracy of which he had dreamed would never come true. Nevertheless, Reimarus insisted, the abiding relevance of the message of Jesus was not dependent on this vain hope, nor was it vitiated by the tragedy of the cross. For at its center, that message corresponded to the best that had been taught by all the saints and sages of human history, and to the deepest intuitions of the human heart; and therefore it was eternal.

The most striking difference between the picture drawn by Reimarus and Jefferson's interpretations, however, was in the mode of their dissemination. For although, as Dumas Malone points out in his magisterial biography,

Jefferson "made no effort to clarify his own position or make his personal religious opinions known [because] ... he regarded this as a wholly private matter which was nobody's business but his," he did not on the other hand attempt to keep the radical Deism of his theological views secret. By contrast, Reimarus remained a closet Deist all his life. He published a mildly rationalistic defense of more or less traditional beliefs about "natural religion," while at the same time he was secretly writing his iconoclastic portrait of Jesus the failure. Only after his death did portions of the work see the light of day, through the efforts of the German philosopher and man of letters, Gotthold Ephraim Lessing (1729–81), who published them between 1774 and 1778 as anonymous "fragments" from the library at Wolfenbüttel. There were, of course, obvious political reasons for this difference between the publication of the two reconstructions of Gospel tradition. Even in the Protestant Germany of the *Aufklärung* there would have been great professional and economic risk if a professor of Hebrew at the University of Hamburg had gone public with such extreme views. Jefferson was running considerably less risk in America, although, as he discovered in his campaigns for the presidency, it was still politically dangerous to be a theological heretic. At the same time, it also bears noting that the posthumous publication of the work of Reimarus created a major stir among theologians and scholars, in a way that the "amateurish" work of his younger and more famous contemporary in Monticello did not.

The "natural religion" that so preoccupied both Reimarus and Jefferson was also a theme to which David Hume gave frequent and careful attention. In Jefferson's judgment, to be sure, his contemporary David Hume did not belong to what he called the "trinity of the three greatest men the world has ever produced," namely, Sir Francis Bacon, Sir Isaac Newton, and John Locke (all three of them British, by the way); for it was these three who had "laid the foundation of those superstructures which have been raised in the physical and moral sciences." Hume's *Dialogues Concerning Natural Religion*—which, like the *Apology* of Reimarus, was published posthumously—probed the attempts to use human reason and experience as the foundation for a consistent interpretation of the world and of God as "a necessarily existent being," as the philosophical theologians of the Enlightenment had been articulating it. The presumption of human reason in asserting "the moral attributes of the Deity, his justice, benevolence, mercy, and rectitude, to be of the same nature with these virtues in human creatures" was sheer "anthropomorphism." Much of the polemic in Hume's *Dialogues Concerning Natural Religion* was specifically aimed at "the ignorance of these reverent gentlemen" among the clergy who continued to make such presumptuous claims for the apologetic enterprise as a prop for orthodox Christian doctrine. But by the time Hume had finished his devastating critique of these claims, he had no less thoroughly disposed of Enlightenment rationalism. Indeed, as he added in a footnote, "it seems evident, that the dispute between the sceptics and dogmatists is entirely verbal."

And that would seem to be an attack no less upon Jefferson's kind of rationalism than upon that of his more orthodox opponents. As has already been suggested, Jefferson was proceeding here in *The Life and Morals of Jesus of Nazareth* on a twofold assumption, which he believed to be ultimately a single assumption: that it was possible, on the basis of reason and without recourse to the notion of special revelation, to know those few universal truths about God and the world and the relation between them that were necessary for a responsible moral life; and that the wisest teachers of the human race, among whom Jesus of Nazareth was preeminent if not unique, had known and promulgated these truths, even though their disciples and followers had often intermingled "dung" with these "diamonds." Because Jefferson was so sure of the first of these assumptions, he could be as confident as he was in applying the second to the Gospels. But if Hume was right in questioning the logical validity of a rationally demonstrable "natural religion," the use of it as a touchstone for sorting out the deeds and sayings of the Gospel tradition must also come into question. Among Christian theologians, especially on the European Continent, Immanuel Kant's (1724–1804) continuation and clarification of Hume's insights into the limitations of reason was in many ways more influential; but taken together, their analyses would make increasingly difficult the simplistic hermeneutical procedures to which Jefferson resorted in his version of "the quest of the historical Jesus."

Theologically the most influential of all of Jefferson's contemporaries on the European Continent was, if not Immanuel Kant, then almost certainly Johann Wolfgang von Goethe. Throughout the rest of the nineteenth century, his philosophy of nature and art permeated the systems of writers and thinkers—"Dichter und Denker"—throughout the West. It was

162

Goethe's bust that Ralph Waldo Emerson put on his mantel, Goethe's *Theory of Colours* (translated into English) that J. M. W. Turner annotated about 1840 as he was working out his own doctrines of color and light, Goethe's conclusion to *Faust* that V. S. Soloviev (arguably the greatest of all Russian philosophers) printed as the epigraph for one of his most important books. And Goethe shared with Jefferson the effort to combine a specific reverence for "the life and morals of Jesus of Nazareth" with a universalism about the strivings and achievements of the human spirit that could not confine its loyalty to any single teacher, not even to Jesus.

The universalism came to voice throughout Goethe's vast authorship, but above all in *Faust*, which opens like the Book of Job and closes like Dante's *Paradiso*, using the old legend of the sorcerer Faust to affirm the human quest for salvation and meaning—but a salvation and meaning available to all who would, by their striving, assert and fulfill their essential humanity. Like Jefferson in his recension of the Gospels, Faust found the story of the resurrection of Jesus unbelievable, attractive though it might be, but retained an eschatological hope for an *apokatastasis pantōn* ("restoration of all things") in which everyone could share. *Faust* is

163

the account of a compact with the Devil for the sake of knowledge and pleasure, but its denouement is a triumph over the Devil and a redemption from sin and error, in which the innocent suffering of Gretchen and the power of her intercession save her betrayer from the consequences of his own folly: "Everything transient is only a parable, the Eternal Feminine leads us upward."

Hovering over that closing scene of Goethe's *Faust* is the mystical figure of Mary—"Virgin, Mother, Queen, Goddess!"—but the figure of Jesus is much more difficult to identify. Yet Goethe's preoccupation with the figure of Jesus was, quite literally, lifelong. On 11 March 1832, just eleven days before his death, Goethe declared in his *Conversations with Eckermann:* "Beyond the grandeur and the moral elevation of Christianity, as it sparkles and shines in the Gospels, the human mind will not advance." Traditional Christianity had sought to preserve that sense of grandeur by encasing the Jesus of the Gospels in the christological dogma of the two natures, as confessed by the Council of Chalcedon in 451. But Goethe, like his slightly older contemporary Jefferson, was convinced that this grandeur, "as it sparkles and shines in the Gospels," was self-authenticating and that it did not need the artificial props of creed, dogma, and liturgy.

Quite the opposite view was espoused by Jefferson's and Goethe's far younger contemporary, John Henry Newman, whose life spanned almost the entire nineteenth century. He, too, was endlessly fascinated by "the grandeur and the moral elevation of Christianity, as it sparkles and shines in the Gospels"; but for him, as he acknowledged in his *Apologia pro vita sua*, "from the age of fifteen dogma has been the fundamental principle of my religion: I know no other religion." Newman was well aware of the literary and historical problems in the composition, collection, and interpretation of the books of the Bible. He also knew, not only historically and philosophically but existentially, the meaning and the power of doubt as a pervasive force in the human mind, and he formulated his most profound and subtle book, *An Essay in Aid of a Grammar of Assent*, as an argument for the compatibility of authentic faith with the lack of the kind of absolute intellectual certainty to which, in traditional apologetics, it is often tied. What brought them together was the reality and power of the Church and of its developing tradition, as that tradition had expressed itself in the Gospels and as it would go on expressing itself in the very creed, dogma, and liturgy that Jefferson found so distasteful.

In that same work, Newman also took up, in an argument with the famous discussion about the causes of the success of Christianity in Edward Gibbon's *The Decline and Fall of the Roman Empire*, what he himself believed to be the central explanation of that success: the Image of Christ, as a principle of association which brings his followers together into the Church as the Body of Christ, and also as the foundation of their moral life. "It was," Newman concluded against Gibbon, "the Thought of Christ, not a corporate body or a doctrine, which inspired that zeal which the historian so poorly comprehends; and it was the Thought of Christ which gave a life to the promise of that eternity, which without Him would be, in any soul, nothing short of an intolerable burden." From that perspective, of course, the wedge that Jefferson sought to drive between the historical Jesus and his followers in succeeding generations was unthinkable: the only Jesus to whom we have access is the Christ of the Church, the Gospels were compiled in the light of the faith of the Church, and the dogma and liturgy of the Church are the key to the faithful interpretation of "the life and morals of Jesus of Naz-

166

areth." Even the gainsayers of dogma would not have the Gospels they use as weapons against it if those Gospels had not been faithfully preserved by the Church.

These similarities and differences between Jefferson and his contemporaries are a testimony to the hold that the figure of the Man in the Gospels continues to have over human hearts and minds, but they also provide a perspective on the heart and mind of one bold and sensitive man who, in his own special way, also wanted to be this Man's disciple and contemporary.

Index OF EXTRACTS

FROM THE NEW TESTAMENT

169

JOHN